Black
in the
Saddle
Again

ALSO BY ARTHUR BLACK

Basic Black

Back to Black

That Old Black Magic

Arthur! Arthur!

Black by Popular Demand

Blackmail! (with Lynne Raymond)

ARTHUR BLACK

Black

in the

Saddle

Again

Published in 1996 by
Stoddart Publishing Co. Limited
34 Lesmill Road
Toronto, Canada
M3B 2T6
Tel. (416) 445-3333
Fax (416) 445-5967

Stoddart Books are available for bulk purchase for sales promotions,
premiums, fundraising, and seminars. For details, contact the
Special Sales Department at the above address.

Canadian Cataloguing in Publication Data

Black, Arthur
Black in the saddle again

ISBN 0-7737-2994-1

1. Canadian wit and humor (English).*   I. Title.

PS8553.L318B52 1996   C818'.5402   C96-931245-8
PR9199.3.B53B52   1996

Cover Design: the boy 100
Text Design: Tannice Goddard

Printed and bound in Canada

Richard Lederer's *Anguished English* quoted with permission
of Wyrick & Company, copyright 1987 by Richard Lederer.

*Stoddart Publishing gratefully acknowledges the support of the
Canada Council and the Ontario Arts Council in the development
of writing and publishing in Canada.*

My thanks to the Canadian Broadcasting Corporation,

Global Television, and the newspapers of Canada

who broadcast and print my humble ramblings.

Contents

3
You Were Saying?   **79**

4
Media Massage   *113*

5

Destination: Anybody's Guess   *139*

6

The World Around Us   *167*

1

It's a Weird, Wired World

Felonious Follies

The most common question people ask when they find out that I scribble for a living is "where do you get your ideas?"

I always tell them that I steal them. Which is true. I steal my column ideas from books, magazines, TV programs, things I see on the street, conversations I deliberately overhear in the supermarket.

Unfortunately, sometimes even theft isn't enough. Every once in a while, a guy will find himself hunched over his word processor, a deadline dangling like a Damoclean switchblade over his neck, his fingers poised like twitchy talons over the keyboard and . . .

Nothing.

No inspiration, no ideas — not even the ghost of a notion to fill the blank gaze of the monitor before him.

Scary . . . but all is not lost.

There's always the Dumb Crooks file to fall back on.

It's a manila folder that I keep beside my desk, bulging with news clippings about ruined robberies, fouled-up felonies, heists gone haywire, and gormless gangsters gang agley.

The daily papers are full of them — tiny little "filler" stories about would-be crooks whose walk on the wild side turned into a pratfall.

Such as? Well, such as the story out of Fort Erie, Ontario. A woman working late in an accounting office looked up to see a man armed with a club. He demanded money, then ordered the woman to get into her car.

She did.

He waited for her to unlock the passenger door.

She didn't.

Instead, the woman drove straight to the police station. The cops immediately issued a bulletin in which the details were a bit sketchy.

Officers were alerted to be on the lookout for a man who was "not too swift."

Speaking of Not Too Swift — how about Donald M. Thomas? Mister Thomas escaped from jail in California after serving eighty-nine days.

Of a ninety-day sentence.

He was captured. He now faces up to twenty years in prison.

Ah, yes, but he'll go down as a Legend of Crime. As the Birdbrain of Alcatraz.

And let us never forget the famous Edmonton Two — a couple of Albertan Butch and Sundance wanna-bes who made Canadian criminal history of a sort the night they knocked over the Petro Canada gas station just outside Vancouver. They surprised the attendant, tied him up, and left him in the washroom, and then escaped with the contents of the till.

But they were, as I say, from Edmonton, and a little bewildered by the bright lights of Vancouver. Which is why, twenty minutes later, they pulled into a gas station to ask directions.

A . . . Petro Canada . . . gas station.

The same Petro Canada station they'd knocked over earlier.

The station attendant, just removing the last of the ropes from his ankles, looked up to see his worst nightmare happening all over again. "I guess they didn't recognize me or the station."

He stammered out directions, then quickly called the cops. Just as he was hanging up, the attendant looked up and saw . . .

the same two guys coming towards him.

Their car wouldn't start. Could the mechanic . . . ? Alas, the mechanic wouldn't be on duty until 8:00 a.m.

The Edmonton Two were waiting for a tow truck when a police cruiser pulled in and graciously offered them a free ride downtown.

Let's give the last word to Thomas Russell in the San Joaquin County Jail. Mister Russell, who was doing time for burglary, was startled to receive a government cheque for $26,447. Startled, but not paralyzed. He immediately used $6,500 to post his own bail and promptly left town with the remaining twenty grand.

Which no doubt really ticked off the San Joaquin County tax collector. He'd sent the cheque to the wrong Thomas Russell.

Not exactly a story of dumb crooks, you say? True.

But the bad guys have to win one once in a while.

4

I Know Your Name, But I Can't Remember Your Face

So there we were, my boon companion and I, tooling along a back road with the windows down and an Arrogant Worms cassette unspooling on the tape deck. It was a Saturday afternoon, one of those last glorious golden fall afternoons you get before the mercury bottoms out and the snow flies.

It was perfect. We had the whole afternoon before us, there wasn't a vehicle on the road, the tires were singing, the trees were undressing . . . Suddenly I swacked my forehead with my palm, straight-legged the brake pedal, and fishtailed to the side of the road.

Boon companion inquired gently as to whether it was the old war wound. No, I said, I just remembered that at that moment I was supposed to be signing books in a bookstore in Kitchener. Which lay about forty-five miles in the opposite direction. There was no excuse. I'd had reminders from the bookstore. I'd even written a little note to myself. I hadn't mistaken, misread, or misunderstood the arrangement. I had simply . . . forgotten about it.

Well, it wasn't too bad, as it turned out. I made it about an hour late and my bookstore hosts, civilized to a fault, even gave me smiles and hot apple cider instead of the reaming out I deserved. But it bothers me, this forgetfulness thing.

Last month I sat through two acts of a Noël Coward play at Niagara-on-the-Lake . . . enjoying it for sure, but with an eerie feeling of déjà vu. Along about the hour-and-a-half mark, it suddenly dawned on me. I'd seen this play before. And only two years before at that.

It could be worse. There's a story about Irwin Edman, a professor of philosophy at Columbia University, well-known for his forgetfulness.

One day he stopped a student on the campus saying, "Pardon me, Hoskins — am I walking north or south?"

"North, professor," answered the student.

"Ah," replied Edman, "then I've had my lunch."

Actors, despite the job requirement of learning lines, are not immune to bouts of amnesia. Richard Burton used to tell a story about one of his pals, a British character actor named Wilfrid Lawson. Lawson invited Burton to see a play that he, Lawson, was appearing in, and since Lawson didn't have to be on stage for a while, he sat down next to Burton to watch the opening scenes. Scene One went by, Scene Two, then Scene Three . . . and Burton was getting a little nervous because Lawson showed no signs of getting up to go backstage. Then suddenly Lawson tapped Burton excitedly on the arm.

"You'll like this bit," whispered Lawson triumphantly. "This is where I come in."

It doesn't usually help to try to finesse your way out of a forgetful situation either. Sir Thomas Beecham, the British conductor, could remember entire scores note for note — but he was hopeless when it came to putting names to faces. Once, in the lobby of a London hotel, he encountered an Imperial-looking woman who seemed familiar, but damned if he could think of her name. He chatted warily with her for a few moments, when it suddenly came to him that he remembered hearing she had a brother. Hoping to connect the dots, Sir Thomas asked, "And your brother . . . is he still well? Still on the same job?"

"Oh, he's veddy well," the woman replied, "and still King of England."

We Snore on Guard for Thee, Baby

There's an old snatch of doggerel that goes:

> *Late last night I slew my wife*
> *Laid her on the parquet flooring*
> *I was loath to take her life*
> *But I had to stop her snoring.*

Ah, yes . . . snoring. Perhaps the greatest single factor in the soaring demand for earplugs and separate bedrooms. Not to mention .38 Smith & Wessons under the pillow. We don't know a lot about snoring, except that it drives non-snorers to fantasies of extreme brutality.

Correction.

We know two or three things about snoring, all of them as baffling as the condition itself. We know, as Mark Twain observed, "there ain't no way to find out why a snorer can't hear himself snore."

We know that between any two bed partners, the snorer is invariably the one who falls asleep first . . .

And we know that nine times out of ten — sorry, fellas — it's us. It's a medically verified fact that men snore far more often than women. So it's not surprising that women have come up with most of the cures.

Swimmers' noseplugs are frequently recommended — or, in an emergency, a good old-fashioned clothespin to the schnozz. I've heard of wives sewing tennis balls onto the backs of their husbands' pyjamas or nightshirts, the theory being that most snoring occurs when the culprit is lying on his back. A spiritually advanced acquaintance of mine says that in the snore wars, she's always favoured superhuman patience, simple understanding, and a work sock stuffed into her hubby's buccal cavity. My boon companion tends to rely on a swift, Gordie Howe–like elbow to the unprotected spleen. They're all decent enough emergency countermeasures, I suppose, but they treat the symptom, not the disease.

And now it turns out that there might not even be a disease. A paleoanthropologist by the name of Carole Anderson Travis has come up with a new theory that indicates snoring is not some disgusting slack-jawed primordial throwback. On the contrary, she says, snoring is decent, honourable, and even brave.

Travis traces the habit back 5 million years, to the time when our ancestors came down out of the trees, coalesced into timid tribes, and took their first tentative steps out onto the veldts and savannahs. Travis theorizes that those first nights on the ground would have been terrifying for our ancestors, with strange unknown predators howling and snarling in the darkness.

To ward off the unseen carnivores, she says, the early humans mimicked the sound of the creatures themselves. Panthers, tigers, hyenas . . . They were sending out a message that said, in effect, "We are carnivores, we are many, we are strong, and we could be hungry!"

So, fellas, the next time you're jolted awake with a kick in the calf or a pillow over the ear, remind your loved one that you're only doing your job, protecting hearth and home from wandering sabre-tooths.

If you're really convincing, she might even give you your half of the blanket back.

Men and Women: Patent Pending

One of my all-time favourite poems — partly because it's one of the all-time shortest poems — is from the pen of Erica Jong. It goes:

> *Men and women; women and men*
> *It will never work.*

Sometimes I think Erica Jong is right. Times like . . . well, when I'm talking to Ian Brown. Ian is a part-time author and full-time bright guy who's written a book called *Man Overboard*, which is about what it's like to be a guy in the nineties. In the book, Ian basically "hangs out" with a lot of fairly unconventional nineties males, and reports on what he sees, hears, and smells. Some of the fellas he fraternized with were decidedly unusual — guys like big game hunters, small-time crooks, pornographic movie stars, and dedicated skirt chasers.

Ian told me about the experience of discussing his book with Peter Gzowski live on CBC's radio program "Morningside." He and Gzowski were humming along when he noticed a lot of waving and gesticulation and wild expressions through the studio glass. He found out later the folks in the control room were frantically fielding phone calls from outraged women.

Ian Brown and Peter Gzowski were having this nice chummy man-to-man and the CBC switchboard was lit up like a runway at Pearson International. "Get this revolting man off the air" was the gist of the calls. "He does not represent modern males. We do not wish to hear his pathetic antediluvian views. Stop his mouth. Now."

Well, geez. The reaction makes Brown sound like some kind of a Machiavellian macho monster, but if you read *Man Overboard*, you encounter a guy who is . . . bewildered, mainly. Just like the rest of us.

9

Just like I was one Christmas, going through the glass door of a downtown bank. I had reached the door in pretty much of a dead heat with a woman in a red coat . . . I don't know what came over me. Call it misguided Yuletide goodwill, call it paranoid patriarchal patronization, call it temporary insanity, but I . . .

held the door open for her.

Naturally, she let me have it with both barrels. The stare, the glare, the smirk, the snarl. "Oh thank you, kind sir, but believe it or not I am perfectly capable of opening my own doors, thank you very much."

Yeah, but . . . I just . . . I didn't . . . I only . . . Oh, never mind.

Garrison Keillor is another Certified Bewildered nineties guy. He believes that women are more qualified to run the world than men. Well, he doesn't go that far. He says women are more qualified to lead an adult life than we are. He says they should go ahead and take over the world holus-bolus, so that "guys can pursue their destiny as adventurers, lovers, humorists and backup singers." I could live with that.

And if I wasn't already spoken for, I think maybe I could live with Robin James, too. Don't know much about Robin, aside from the fact that she recently wrote the following letter to the editor of the *New York Times*.

"I was walking to my office the other morning," she wrote, "and found myself caught in an unusual verbal crossfire. A group of workmen noted my existence with whistles and other such noises.

"A more politically correct gentleman unloading a truck on the other side of the street called out in a broad New York accent: 'Hey, guys, relax. It's just a woman.'

"Thanks, I guess." Signed, Robin James.

Hey, Robin? Arthur here. Men and women . . . women and men. Do you think it could ever work?

A Little Salad
with Your Night
Crawlers, Sir?

So the story as I understand it goes like this. A teacher in Ottawa is in hot water because he feeds worms to his class. He didn't force or trick them to eat worms. The parents were informed by letter. The kids were allowed to make up their own minds whether to chow down or not. The worms were clean and chemical-free and tastefully presented — boiled for just a few minutes and served with lemon wedges.

So what's the fuss? It's not the first time wiggly squigglys have passed human lips. Ask Rusty Rice of Rialto College, California. Rusty holds the world title for worm eating, having forked up twenty-eight of the critters at a sitting a few years back. Not the first time worms have figured in haute cuisine, either. The top prize winner in a cooking competition not too long ago was a recipe for Earthworm Applesauce Surprise Cake. I don't think it entirely spoils the story to know that the competition was sponsored by the North American Bait Company.

Listen — strip worms of their stereotype and they're kind of attractive, foodwise. They're boneless. You don't have to pluck them. Or scale or de-talon or flense, fillet, or stuff them. Mexicans just grill 'em up like bacon strips and serve 'em on toast. In Japan a lot of old fellas drink a potion made from earthworms for its aphrodisiac properties. And before you wrinkle your nose and go GAAAAAH!, take a look at North America's Menu du Jour.

We belong to a culture that thinks nothing of taking great ugly underwater behemoths that look like leftovers from a space horror movie — lobsters, I'm talking about — plopping them on a plate, then dismantling them right there on the dinner table. We are a people that boil up and nibble at the artichoke, a treacherous, mind-numbing foodstuff, the eating of which is about as much fun as licking 1,100 forty-five-cent stamps in a row. We eat parsley, which Ogden Nash pronounced gharsley. Rightly, I think.

And broccoli. Which is perhaps the one subject on which George Bush and I agree. Me, George, and Roy Blount Junior, actually. Mister Blount wrote a broccoli song once, the lyrics of which go: "The neighbourhood stores are all out of broccoli. Loccoli."

And what about oysters? What can you say about an assemblage of tastebuds that would lever a homely old oyster out of the seabed wrack and muck, winkle its barnacle-crusted shell open, and crow, "Hot dog! A brand new taste sensation!" When it comes to oysters, I'm with Miss Piggy, who once sniffed: "I simply cannot imagine why anyone would eat something slimy served on an ashtray."

Oh, I know there are a lot of oyster lovers out there, and that's fine. A lot of folks, believe it or not, find my favourite sandwich — peanut butter, marmalade, sliced Spanish onion with a light sprinkling of Worcestershire sauce — unpalatable. That's fine, too. There's no accounting for human taste. We just have to be careful about turning up our noses when new food ideas like, well, worms, come along. After all, the food fad of the eighties was sushi. Uncooked fish.

A Mexican comedian once told his English-speaking audience. "Down in Mexico we have a word for sushi. Bait."

Which, when you think about the kids eating worms in Ottawa, kind of brings us full circle, doesn't it?

On the Job

"Work" . . . what a funny word when you think about it. Not that much different from the ancient "verk" — which some acquisitive Anglo-Saxon copped from the Old Norse language several hundred years ago.

Strange word for a strange concept. Some pretty good minds have tried to define the phenomenon. The philosopher Bertrand Russell declared that there are only two kinds of work. Number one: altering the position of matter at or near the earth's surface, relative to other matter. And number two: telling other people to do it. Ogden Nash nailed down another important work characteristic. "People who work sitting down," observed Nash, "get paid more than people who work standing up."

Unless you happen to work at hitting baseballs for a living.

You wouldn't think a four-letter epithet like work could cradle so many contradictions. We've got works of art, bridgework, men at work, work to rule, off work. That's the really weird thing about work. We mumble and moan endlessly about having to go to work . . . while secretly praying that we'll never be out of it.

What is this human foible? Antelope don't work. Turkey vultures make their own hours. Your weeniest microbe may be voteless and unsexy and not very bright — but at least it doesn't have to go to work for a living.

Not like we do. Nine to five, day shift, night shift, time and a half for overtime, forty hours a week, forty-eight weeks a year, not counting Christmas, New Year's, and statutory holidays.

Very odd. Most of us spend better than half our waking hours "at work," and getting to and from it, for five of the seven days we get each week. Which is to say we work more than we sleep or eat or read or make love or hang out with friends.

And why is it we are doing this again? I keep forgetting. Oh right, to become wealthy so we don't have to work. Well, I don't know about you but I've been at it pretty steadily for four decades, and wealth has never been further off. I had more money in my pocket when I was a pin boy at the bowling alley.

Work. We gripe and we groan about it; we shirk and slough it off and try to get out of as much of it as we can, but my, don't we wax self-righteous when we see somebody who's managed to hacksaw their way free of the work ethic ball and chain?

Welfare bums. Pogey cheats. Shiftless good for nothings. HEY YA BUM . . . GET A JOB!

The writer Richard Needham had a theory about that. "If you enjoy your work," he wrote, "you don't mind other people not working; in fact, you're happy to support them. But if, like most Canadians, you hate your work, you resent seeing anybody idle. You want everyone to be as miserable as you are."

Aha. That's the cushy job we're all looking for, of course. Once you like what you're doing, it stops being work. Archibald Lampman put it quite elegantly: "Work is only toil when it is the performance of duties for which nature did not fit us, and a congenial occupation is merely serious play."

But what about the dignity of labour? Summed up nicely, I think, in an anecdote they tell about JFK when he was campaigning for the presidential nomination in West Virginia, back in 1960. At one stop, Kennedy was confronted by a hollow-eyed man, all bone and gristle and coal smudges — obviously a miner. "It true yore the son o' one of ar richest men?" the miner demanded. Kennedy nodded, warily. "True you never wanted for anythin' and had everythin' you wanted?" continued the miner, his eyes boring in.

"I guess so," admitted Kennedy.

"It true you never done a day's work with yore hands all the days of yore life?" accused the miner.

Kennedy nodded guiltily again.

"Well let me tell you somethin', son," growled the miner. "You . . . haven't missed a thing."

You're Not Getting Better, You're Getting Older

You know the most sobering thing I've heard in a while? It was comedian Gary Shandling, hosting some music awards — the Grammies or the Grampies or the Junos or the Mayos, I don't remember what the show was, but I remember what Shandling said.

"These are scary times," Shandling remarked. "We live in an age when Mick Jagger is older than the president of the United States."

I never thought of that. More important, I never thought of the corollary: *I'M* older than the president of the United States. I can't balance a chequebook and I've had more chance to practise than Bill Clinton. What are his chances of wrestling the *national debt* to a draw?

What Gary Shandling was really confronting was Middle Age. A mysterious period. A nebulous time of life with no set annular rings to mark it out. When I was a kid, I believed that Middle Age began at about thirty . . . but now that I'm over fifty I realize I was way off . . .

Hard to say exactly when Middle Age sets in. One duffer decided that it's that time of your life when you realize you're too young to take up golf but too old to rush the net.

The American humorist Calvin Trillin put it this way:

"When someone reaches Middle Age, people he knows begin to get put in charge of things, and knowing what he knows about the people who are being put in charge of things scares the hell out of him."

Well, it was something like that that scared the hell out of me. It was a thing called Wayne Gretzky. I remember when Wayne Gretzky was a downy-cheeked, teenage phenom. Then my newspaper apprised me of what a tough time Gretzky was having. The reporter even speculated that at the end of the (1993) season, "the grizzled veteran may hang up his skates for good."

Grizzled veteran?????? Wayne Gretzky is younger than Pacman! Teenage Mutant Ninja Turtles! Cabbage Patch Dolls! Why . . . I was an adult . . . a taxpayer . . . a parent . . . I was *bald* the year Wayne Gretzky turned pro!!!!

And now he's a greybeard? An oldster? A grizzled veteran?

Steady, Black. Take solace in the late achievers. Remember that Winston Churchill wrote *A History of the English Speaking Peoples* when he was eighty-two.

That Coco Chanel opened a fashion firm when she was eighty-five.

That Pablo Casals was giving cello concerts, George Bernard Shaw was writing plays, and Grandma Moses was turning out canvases at the ages of eighty-eight, ninety-three, and one hundred, respectively.

No. Always remember that getting old is nothing to be frightened of.

Besides, it's not as if it sneaks up on you. There are three surefire ways of spotting old age.

One is the loss of memory.

I can't remember the other two.

You Think YOU Have a Weight Problem?

*I've been on a diet for twenty-one days
and all I've lost is three weeks.*

I don't know who said that, but let's face it: chances are pretty good that it could have been you, or me, or that lady over there with her nose pressed flat against the bakery window. Seems like everybody this side of Twiggy is on a diet these days. Or planning to go on one. Or picking themselves up after falling off one.

The statistics are telling. At any given time, 50 percent of North American women are on some diet. Men are only slightly less neurotic about fat — only 30 percent of the males you meet are "cutting back on calories" in one way or another.

And such ways! There are low-cal beverages, "Lite" foods, and a plethora of over-the-counter appetite suppressants. Your friendly neighbourhood bookstore offers a whole flotilla of paperback diet options. You can choose from the Hilton Head, the Hollywood, the Pritikin, the Beverly Hills, and the Drinking Man's Diet, just to name a handful.

And if printed assistance isn't enough, there are always the surgical options: wired jaws, stapled guts, and even liposuction — a.k.a. Diet by Hoover.

But the saddest dieting statistic of all? The fact that after three years, 95 percent of all the people who lose weight on crash diets or through radical surgery *regain every pound they lost* — and usually more.

So let's have some good news. Number one: medical authorities are coming around to the point of view that being a few pounds "overweight" is no big deal — unless you're a fashion model or a jockey.

Number two: You Are Not That Fat. I don't care if your kids call you Jabba the Hut and you haven't seen your toes since World War II.

Let's face it: next to Walter Hudson, you're built like a garter snake. Mister Hudson first made the news back in 1987, when firemen were called to his New York apartment to free him. He was wedged in the doorway to his bathroom.

The firemen must have felt like they'd stumbled into a horror movie. It took nine of them just to lever Walter Hudson back to his specially reinforced bed. They brought in an industrial scale to weigh the man, but it broke down.

The scale only went to 995 pounds.

They got a bigger scale, used for weighing vehicles. They manoeuvred Mister Hudson onto it. The needle showed that Walter Hudson, who was five feet ten inches tall, weighed 1,190 pounds.

Which put Walter Hudson in the *Guinness Book of Records* — and brought him to the attention of Dick Gregory. The black ex-comedian-turned-nutrition-guru flew to Walter Hudson's bedside and vowed that he would help the man return to normal size.

Dick Gregory made good on his claim, too. Over the next two years, thanks to a special diet devised by Gregory, Walter Hudson melted off an unbelievable 670 pounds.

Imagine — the guy shed the weight of four normal-sized men!

So here's Walter Hudson at a relatively svelte 520 pounds — able to walk and go outside and lead a normal life after three decades of crippling fatness. Did he live happily ever after?

Alas, no. Walter Hudson fell off the diet wagon. In less than a year he nibbled his way back up almost to the level that got him in the *Guinness Book of Records* as the heaviest living human.

But Walter wasn't living any more. He died in 1992 of a heart attack at the age of forty-six.

And when they rolled his body into the Nassau County Morgue, it tipped the scales at 1,125 pounds.

Would You Care
To Buttle?

*An aristocracy . . . is like a chicken with its head cut off; it
may run about in a lovely way, but in fact it's dead.*

NANCY MITFORD

Ms. Mitford is right, of course. Kings and queens and dukes and
duchesses would make no sense at all in a rational world.

But then, when's the last time anybody mistook Earth for a rational
planet?

This is a place where religious leaders can solemnly order the murder of a man for writing a book.

It's a place where a guy can earn $5 million U.S. a year for throwing
a leather-covered sphere past another guy sixty-six feet away.

This is a place that picked Brian Mulroney to run Canada.

Twice.

So perhaps it's no surprise that Ivor Spencer's enterprise is doing
swimmingly well, thank yew veddy much.

Mister Spencer runs a school in London, England. A school for
butlers.

A person might be forgiven for thinking that butlers had gone the
way of the brontosaurus, the dodo, and the Edsel. Back in the 1930s
there were thirty thousand of the creatures in Britain alone, but World
War II cost Britain mightily, and butlers — an expensive appendage
during the best of times — began to disappear. By the 1980s there
were fewer than a hundred full-time butlers in the United Kingdom.

Now they're coming back. Or so says Ivor Spencer — and he's in a
position to know. Mister Spencer's school grooms, hones, and places
"personal servants" with wealthy households all over the world.

It's not a bad gig. About $50,000 a year with free room and board, a car, a clothing allowance, and the chance to serve tea to the rich and famous.

But there's a downside. Rich people are not necessarily nice people — and even when the boss is a twenty-four-carat jerk, the butler is expected to lower his eyes and take it, like a good and loyal servant. A butler is unflinchingly stiff-upper-lipped. His employer can get drunk, shout obscenities, beat the dog, and swing naked from the chandeliers, but nary a whisper of it will be breathed by his butler.

"We never talk," says Spencer. "That is your death knell as a butler."

Which is not to say that butlers are a bunch of craven, lickspittle doormats shuffling and cringing through life. Some of them have immense responsibilities, which include everything from balancing the family budget to ironing the morning newspaper. A butler may not talk back, but he's nobody's punching bag, either. Indeed, their grace under pressure is legendary.

For instance, the butler of Lord Dunsany in County Meath, Ireland. Back in the 1920s, Dunsany Castle was raided and ransacked by the "Black and Tans" — troops of the British government. Lord Dunsany's butler stood unmoved as the soldiers reduced the castle interior to rubble. As they trooped out the smashed front door, the butler intoned, "Who shall I say called?"

Then there's the New York mansion story told by Cobourg, Ontario's own Marie Dressler in her autobiography, *My Own Story*. "I was going upstairs to leave my wrap when I noticed a beautifully carved bannister. 'If I don't slide down that,' I told myself, 'I'll die.' There was nobody in sight. I took a deep breath and landed in a heap at the foot of the stairs. Imagine my horror when I saw bearing down upon me the butler, whose frosty hauteur had frozen me when I arrived. He picked me up and dusted me off without a flicker of expression on his correct countenance, meanwhile murmuring cordially, 'Very good, miss. Very good indeed. I've always wanted to take a go at it myself.'"

Champion Cheapskates

It's official — this rotten, cash-draining, hope-deflating, dream-postponing recession that has dogged our staggering footsteps for the past few years is finally over!

The prime minister says so.

Statistics Canada says so.

Even the *Globe and Mail* Report on Business says so. Isn't that great? Well, maybe.

Or maybe the Canadian media, in their role as an upbeat, positive-thinking agency, are just doing their best to lever their readers over that ice ridge known as the midwinter blahs.

Statistics Canada's end-of-recession pronouncement? You know what Benjamin Disraeli said: "There are three kinds of lies: lies, damned lies, and statistics."

As for the prime minister, well, let's just say that prime ministers have been known to fib before.

Call me a pessimistic curmudgeon, but I'm not leaving the fallout shelter just yet. I don't truly believe this recession is over.

And even if it is — how long do we have before another "economic downturn" rumbles down the pike to kick us in the assets?

What's more, if I'm right and all the aforementioned optimistic soothsayers in the rose-coloured bifocals are wrong — I don't think it's such a bad thing.

There's a positive side to life in a recession. It forces us to resurrect one of the cardinal virtues for which Canadians are world-renowned.

It reminds us of the importance of Thinking Cheap.

You didn't know Canucks are thrifty? Come on. We're so tight we squeak when we walk.

A Canuck is a guy who will give you the sleeves off his vest.

Did you know the limbo dance is not a Caribbean invention? It was actually invented right here, north of the 49th.

By a Canuck trying to get into a pay toilet for free.

Nope, we Great White Northerners are cheap and what's more, we're good at it. At least we used to be. Canadians fell into some profligate habits during the seventies and eighties. That's why the recession hit us like a schoolmarm's rap across the knuckles.

A few years ago (before the recession descended), I decided to find out just how cheap my fellow citizens were. So I asked my radio show listeners to nominate the cheapest person they knew. In other words, the Tightest Wad on the Tundra.

The cards and letters poured in. Many of them stamped "insufficient postage."

A skinflint from Rothesay, New Brunswick, wrote: "I always take a plastic fly with me to a restaurant. After eating my meal I call the waitress over and point to the critter on my plate. Ninety-nine point nine percent of the time you don't have to pay after she sees it on the crust."

A miser from Saskatoon confessed: "On really cold winter days I used to spit on a nickel . . . shove it in a parking meter . . . turn the handle and freeze the meter for the whole day — eight hours of parking for five cents."

Some Canucks are so thrifty they even get their sexual titillation second-hand. A listener from Whitehorse wrote: "My husband pores over the brassiere ads in the Sears Catalogue because he's too cheap to buy *Playboy*. This is called Yukon Porn."

And my favourite — a cheapskate from Oklee, Minnesota, wrote: "When special occasions arrive, i.e., Christmas, birthdays, anniversaries, et cetera, my wife and I go to the Greeting Card store, select the cards of our choice for one another, read them and then return them to the display."

That's the kind of lesson we can learn from a recession! That's the kind of spirit that made this country great!

Now if you'll excuse me, I promised to meet my wife downtown at the drug store. It's kind of a special date — her birthday, as a matter of fact. I'm treating her to an evening at the Hallmark Card rack.

Long John Silver
Was a Wimp

Don't talk to me. Don't even look at me. I'm in a bad mood.

I've just had one of my all-time favourite myths pulverized like a sea biscuit under Long John Silver's peg leg.

That's the very myth I mean — pirates. It probably indicates a mutant chromosome in my genetic balance sheet, but I've always had a perverse fascination with pirates. I liked pirates because in a world of shifting values, weasel words, and fake imagery — pirates were, at least, real.

Real . . . *bad.*

The baddest, in fact. Nastier than Nazis and more ruthless than lawyers, even. Pirates had no redeeming features. We're talking about thugs who stalked fat, unarmed merchant ships. Who gloated as they slaughtered unarmed crews and passengers. Who boozed and raped and pillaged and plundered and sent anyone who stood in their way for a long stroll off a short plank, right?

Nah. Not even close.

Fact is, we can thank Robert Louis Stevenson and J. M. Barrie for most of the "truths" we know about pirates. Robert Louis Stevenson wrote *Treasure Island.* J. M. Barrie gave us *Peter Pan.*

But based on historical records, it looks like Messrs. Stevenson and Barrie probably couldn't tell a pirate cutlass from a pork cutlet.

First, the famous skull and crossbones flag. Everybody knows that pirates invariably hoisted the old S&C when they were bearing down on some hapless treasure-laden galleon, right? Wrong. Pirates flew red flags, black flags, flags with full skeletons — in short, any damn flags they pleased. For the most part, they ran up the flag of Utmost Convenience. In other words, if a British frigate was their prey, they flew the Union Jack. If it was a French sloop they had in their sights, they made sure the fleur-de-lis was fluttering in the breeze.

The better to bamboozle the quarry, my pretties.

What about the plank, then? Surely the stories about pirates prinking captives off a plank into the briny are true? Not according to Hugh Rankin, author of *The Golden Age of Piracy*. Ye olde plankwalk, writes Rankin, "appears to have been a fabrication of later generations." Rankin says that when pirates wished to rid themselves of enemies, they simply tossed them over the rail — without benefit of diving board.

Turns out that even among themselves, pirates weren't the lawless band of savages we've come to know and loathe. Buccaneer politics weren't anything like the anarchic seadog-eat-seadog frenzy one might have assumed. It was more like . . . well, the United Nations.

David Cordingly is the organizer of an exhibition on pirate history at the National Maritime Museum in London, England. According to him, inter-pirate behaviour was surprisingly charitable. "Pirates were extraordinarily democratic," he says. "Plunder had to be shared out equally. The captain could take a bit more, but not a lot more, unlike the Navy. A pirate crew could even vote their captain out of office."

Cordingly claims that pirates even operated a kind of High Seas Health Plan — losing a leg in battle, for example, guaranteed a bigger share of the booty.

And here's the kicker for me. Care to meet two of the bloodthirstiest pirates of all time? One was a fearless cutthroat named Read; the other, a sadistic swashbuckler named Bonny. Read and Bonny roamed the seas in the early 1700s, separately at first, then together on an English pirate ship under Calico Jack Rackham. Finally, in 1721 a Jamaican warship tracked them down and after a vicious battle in which Read and Bonny were the last to yield, they captured the pirate sloop and threw the whole crew in chains.

The entire crew was tried, found guilty, and hanged. With the exception of Read and Bonny. They were excused.

They were pregnant. Bonny's first name was Anne; Read's was Mary.

Sure throws cold water on the pirate legend. On the other hand, it opens a whole new career option for Sheila Copps.

Justice by the Handful

I hear rumours that Clint Eastwood plans to do another *Dirty Harry* movie.

I can't pretend that I'm surprised. It must be easy work. When he portrays that ne'er-do-well, rogue San Francisco detective, Harry Callaghan, all Clint has to do is squint a lot, adjust his sunglasses from time to time, and blow away bad guys with his .44 Magnum.

I can't say that I'm surprised, either, that *Dirty Harry* movies continue to be box-office dynamite. They flog the same commodity offered by the *Death Wish* movies Charles Bronson sleepwalks through every couple of years — simple, Old Testament solutions to modern problems. In the worlds of *Death Wish* and *Dirty Harry,* the lesson is always cut and dried and the bad guys are always badder than bad. They're scum: ergo, gun them down.

Would that real life were so simple. Would that modern justice were even in the ballpark.

The other day, on my TV, Oprah was interviewing a prison inmate who had just been sentenced for dealing heroin.

"What did the judge give you?" Oprah asked.

"Eighteen years," said the prisoner.

"And when do you get out?" pursued Oprah.

"I'm eligible for parole next summer," the prisoner replied.

And the TV audience *laughed*! That's how cynical we've become about the courts and justice.

That's why a little cheer leaps unbidden to the back of our throats when we see Dirty Harry short-circuit a legal system that's constipated to the point of immobility. Hooray — here comes simple, monosyllabic Harry dispensing instant "justice" in lethal lead capsules. It's stupid. It's fantasy. But it works.

And the news we get from the courts doesn't seem calculated to make Six Gun Justice any less attractive. Some time ago, I wrote about the despondent New Yorker who tried to kill himself by jumping in front of a subway train. He lived — albeit as a quadriplegic. When he recovered sufficiently, the would-be suicide sued the New York Transit Authority for a million dollars, claiming the Authority had failed to protect him.

He won, too.

Not long ago, a woman sued the Chicago rapid transit system over the death of her husband. And how had he died, exactly? Well, while waiting for his train, he urinated over the tracks.

Right on the electrified rail.

The wife sued for neglect, claiming $1.5 million would go a long way towards allaying her grief.

She also won.

Ah, but every so often the universe unfolds the way it ought to. I give you the tale of a would-be Mississippi rapist. One night a man broke into a house in Jackson and found himself in the bedroom of a fifty-year-old unprotected woman.

Perfect!

He jumped on the woman, slapped her around, cursed her, and when he had her thoroughly frightened, took off his clothes. Which is when the woman grabbed him in what would have been an intimate embrace if it hadn't been quite so . . . energetic.

There are no names in jiujitsu for the hold the woman put on the man. You won't see it employed by members of the World Wrestling Federation. Suffice to say it was two-handed, vice-like, and extremely painful.

"Please, please," the man whimpered, "you're killing me!"

"Die, then," the woman said.

"Woman, you got me suffering," he moaned.

"Have you thought about how you were going to leave me suffering?" she replied. With a twist.

The would-be rapist eventually managed to break free and get away, but he wasn't hard to find. Police just followed the crawl marks in the dirt, which led right to his house. They found him in bed, in great pain.

I don't know how Dirty Harry would feel about it, but a story like that sure makes my day.

Winnie's Bar Tab

You like bar stories? Here's a bar story for you. Guy walks into a bar, walks up to the bartender, bartender says, "Ah, we've been waiting for you, sir. Would you be so kind as to take care of this?" And he hands the guy a bill.

Sounds like the start of another dumb bar joke, but this one has a twist. It really happened. Here's a couple more twists to the story. The bar bill was ninety-two years old. It was owed by a British Army lieutenant now deceased . . . plus the guy the bartender presented the bill to was Prince Charles.

It happened in Hyderabad, India, during a royal tour several years ago.

Poor Charles. It's not bad enough he has to endure the incessant yapping of the rumour-mongering press and the flashbulb-popping paparazzi. Not enough that he turns on his TV to discover everyone from Geraldo to Oprah Winfrey casually dissecting his sex life. Now he gets whacked with bar bills left by nineteenth-century British Army deadbeats.

Can't help hoping that the ghost of the long-dead British lieutenant was hovering halfway between the ceiling fan and the royal right shoulder when the bill was presented, though. It would be particularly heavenly, I would think, for a British Tommy to witness his booze chit being picked up by the heir to the Throne.

Personally I've never known a bartender long enough or intimately enough to run a tab. And probably just as well. The whole concept of bar tabs is like alimony to me. Kind of like buying gas for a repossessed car.

Of course, if you have to be in debt there are ways to handle it.

When your credit cards have been recalled and the bailiff's hauled away your stereo, and moths are negotiating condo leases for your wallet . . . when your back is against the financial wall, a little chutzpah never hurts.

Such as that displayed by German playwright Max Halbe, who as a young starving artist often fell behind in his rent. Sneaking into his flat one night, he came face to face with his landlady. "Herr Halbe," she thundered, "you are three months in arrears. If you don't pay up, I shall be forced to evict you."

"Oh don't do that, madame," pleaded Halbe. "Why don't you just raise my rent?"

A turn-of-the-century American versifier by the name of Oliver Herford was even cheekier in a showdown with the manager of the hotel he lived in. Meeting Herford one day in the lobby, the manager frostily inquired whether he had received his latest, long overdue bill.

"Yes," replied Herford.

"And is that all you have to say?" asked the manager.

"At the moment, yes," replied Herford airily, "but if the bill gets any larger, I shall have to ask for a bigger room."

Not that Prince Charles needs any lessons in how to avoid paying other people's debts. When he was presented with the ninety-two-year-old unpaid bar bill, the Prince scrutinized it briefly, smiled, and handed it back, saying, "You've preserved your records very well."

Well, I don't think the management was really serious about collecting the debt. The bill was only for thirteen rupees.

And the signature of the Army lieutenant who ran up the tab made it kind of a keepsake. It read: "Winston Spencer Churchill."

The Dreaded "G" Word

I'm going to warn you right off the top. If you don't care for four-letter words, you'd better turn the page right now.

This piece is devoted to one of the dirtiest four-letter words ever to dog-paddle up to the surface of the semantic cesspool known as the English language.

Still reading? Okay, you asked for it.

This essay is about golf.

The kind of golf I want to talk about goes on year-round, rain or shine, blizzard or drought, day or night.

I'm talking about miniature golf.

Has anyone ever come up with a dopier way to make us while away our excess leisure hours? Can you imagine Alexander the Great or Mary Queen of Scots creeping avidly along a swatch of indoor–outdoor carpeting? Chipping feeble shots off garden gnomes and plastic palm trees? Banking putts off plywood windmills? Driving their balls deep into sand traps the size of bathmats?

Well, perhaps Mary Queen of Scots. The lady was an avid golfer. In fact, legend has it that she was out swatting a few balls just a couple of days after her husband died.

But that's not callous. That's what golfers are like.

There is the story about the golfer who was out on the course with his wife and he came to this ball lying about sixty yards from the fourth hole. Trouble was, there was a huge barn between the ball and the hole. He was about to play around the barn when the caddy said, "Hold on. I believe you could hit your ball through that barn window and clean through the open door on the other side. That should put you right on the green!"

Well, the golfer teed up and let go with a blistering drive. It went screaming through the barn window, caromed off a hay baler, ricocheted off a barn beam, and came straight back out, hitting the golfer's wife right between the eyes and killing her instantly.

Ten years later, the same duffer — older, greyer, sadder, and widowed, but still golfing — found himself in exactly the same situation: sixty yards from the fourth hole, lying in the shadow of the same massive barn.

His caddy said: "Why don't you try hitting your ball through that barn window there? It'd go right through the open door on the other side and put you right on the green!"

The sad old golfer dropped his iron, fell on his knees, and began sobbing uncontrollably. The caddy rushed over to comfort him. "What's the matter?"

"Ten years ago my wife and I were right here," groaned the golfer between sobs, "I had the same shot . . . and I triple-bogeyed the hole!"

But hey, I digress. I want to talk about miniature golf. I especially want to try to figure out why it's so popular.

The game was invented back during World War I at Pigeon Forge, Tennessee. A landowner by the name of James Barber thought it was too hot to walk a full eighteen holes, so he called in some workmen and had them lay out a shrunken course on his front lawn. The madness spread. By 1930, you could find 4 million North Americans on any given night, hunched over their putters on miniature courses around the country. The game celebrated its seventy-fifth birthday a couple of years ago, and it looks like it's more popular than ever.

So what's the attraction? Well, it's easy to be good at miniature golf. You can play with your kids, your granny, a war amp — anybody. You don't have to be a youngster, either. There's a guy in Myrtle Beach who regularly beats the cleats off all comers on one of the town's fifty miniature golf courses. He is ninety-three years old.

Old duffers need mini golf for the day when real golf gets too hard. You heard the story about the two oldsters, Eddie and Moe, who played as a team? Eddie, seventy-six, could drive like a pro, but his eyesight was bad. Moe, eighty-one, couldn't hit worth a darn, but his eyes were as keen as an eagle's. So Eddie tees up and smacks a beauty. And Moe shades his eyes as he watches the ball soar. "Did you see it, Moe?" asks Eddie.

"Yeah," says Moe, "real good."

"Well," says Eddie, "where did it go?"

And Moe pauses for a moment, then says, "I forget."

If Alferd Invites You to Dinner — Don't Go!

The guy in the coffee shop was singing a familiar tune.

"Lookit this mass murderer creep," he growled, pointing a crescent moon of chocolate glazed doughnut at the front page of the tabloid rag on the counter. "Kills people. Eats them. Paints their skulls. Ah, I tell ya."

He went on to grouse about other human horrors of our time. Wayne Gacey. Paul Bernardo. The KGB/CIA/IRA/PLO.

"I'm tellin' ya, I don't know what the world is comin' to," he sermonized to no one in particular.

And then, the kicker:

"Sure wasn't like that in the old days."

He was a big guy, this coffee shop orator. He had one of those wallets on a stainless steel chain attached to his belt, and he cradled his coffee mug in a big meaty mitt that looked like it might bounce off, oh say, the jaw of a smart alec and be little the worse for the adventure.

Otherwise, I'm sure I would have said something.

Something like, "Horsefeathers."

I get a little impatient with folks who try to sell the notion that, depravity-wise, Things Have Never Been So Bad.

The truth is, wickedness has always had a deluxe suite at the Hotel Homo Sapiens. We've had our share of saints, holy folk, and just plain good people over the years, but that same history is pockmarked with ogres and tyrants, murderers and scallywags.

We've got more nosy reporters around these days, that's all.

But perhaps you think I'm all wet. Maybe you're convinced that our parents — or at least our parents' parents — lived in an altogether more innocent time, when people really were the kinder, gentler folk George Bush used to prattle about.

In that case, ladies and gentlemen, allow me to introduce you to Mister Alferd E. Packer.

Yes, "Alferd." Spelling is but one of many of society's secrets Mister Packer failed to unravel in his unhappy meander through Life. Unused to reading or writing, Mister Packer seldom signed his name, but when he did, he spelled it "Alferd."

He led an undistinguished life, did Mister Packer, performing odd jobs that blew him like so much sagebrush back and forth across the American southwest. In the winter of 1874, Fate found Alferd and five companions slogging through a remote valley in the San Juan mountains not far from Lake City, in Hinsdale County, Colorado. The six men were adventurers, westward bound, looking for the proverbial pot of gold.

It was a rough winter with lots of cold and snow. Indians went hungry and whole herds of cattle froze on the hoof. Nobody much expected to see the six men come spring.

And mostly, they were right — five of them never showed up. Just Alferd Packer. A . . . remarkably *well-fed* Alferd Packer, for a man who'd supposedly spent the winter starving in the mountains. After the spring thaw, horrified investigators found Alferd's last camp site. There they discovered the dismembered remains of Alferd's erstwhile companions. They had been murdered with an axe.

And then they had been eaten.

Alferd denied responsibility. Then he confessed to killing one of them in self-defence. Finally he owned up to the whole shebang: multiple murders plus gastronomy above and beyond the boundaries of the Cordon Bleu Cookbook.

It wasn't a pretty case, but I'd have risked upchucking my lunch to have been in that courtroom when District Judge Melville B. Gerry pronounced sentence on the hapless Packer.

Legend has it that the Judge said this:

"Stand up, you man-eatin' sonofabitch. Stand up." Then, the judge thundered: "There was seven Dimmicrats in Hinsdale County and you et five of 'em, damn you. I sentence you to be hanged by the neck until you're dead, dead, dead, as a warning against reducin' the Democratic population of the state."

That's how the legend goes. And if it isn't true, it ought to be.

She's a Man — No, He's a Woman

Ready for another sea change in shopping patterns? This phenomenon is gathering steam in the shopping malls and chic boutiques of sunny California. The *Los Angeles Times* calls it "Cross Shopping."

What's happening is unprecedented numbers of men shopping for women, and women shopping for men — but particularly the former. Los Angeles retailers are reporting whole new herds of males poking around the lingerie and notions departments, where only the female of the species used to congregate.

What's it mean? No one is quite sure. Some experts think men cop an illicit thrill just infiltrating "behind enemy lines." Other behaviourists tug their beards and warn of a dark side to cross shopping — they say it represents an attempt by men to exert control over their spouses.

I say phooey. I don't think there's anything sinister or illicit about cross shopping at all. I believe it represents but one more revolution of the Gender Blender that's been turning us into biological vichyssoise for years.

And about time, too. I come from an age when there were separate entrances at the public schools marked BOYS and GIRLS. I come from an age when all public taverns had a special door marked LADIES AND ESCORTS. I can remember a kid in my grade eight class being sent home in tears. Her crime? She dared to wear slacks to class.

Just to show you how much times have changed, consider the case of Brett Martin, an eighteen-year-old senior high school student in Knoxville, Iowa. He, too, got in hot water for "inappropriate dress" — but with a distinctly nineties twist.

Brett was nailed for showing up at his Knoxville High School prom dressed in a wig, mascara, and a red, sequined, spaghetti-strapped dress he borrowed from his sister.

Brett Martin did it as a lark, but the Knoxville High School principal — a humourless sod who must have been caught sneaking in the GIRLS entrance as a student — didn't laugh. Instead he had Martin charged with criminal trespass.

The principal should get with the times. Hasn't he heard about Teresinha de Jesus Gomes? Teresinha is a hearty, glad-handing fifty-year-old woman who's been famous in military circles of Portugal for the past two decades.

But not as Teresinha de Jesus Gomes.

Her army buddies knew her as Tito Anibal de Paixao Gomes.

Uh, that's *General* Tito Anibal de Paixao Gomes, to be precise.

For nineteen years, "the General" regaled his/her fellow officers with tales of daring military-intelligence-gathering adventures in South America and behind the Iron Curtain.

They were great stories, but that's all they were. Teresinha/Tito had been impersonating an officer since she donned a general's uniform and her dead brother's name away back in 1974. She'd probably still be in the Portuguese Army if she hadn't run up colossal debts for her intended State Wedding. Authorities took away her general's uniform and let her off with a three-year suspended sentence.

Oh yeah, and the wedding is off, too.

But the good times are just starting for Damian Taylor down in Brisbane, Australia. Damian is an Australian lifeguard in his twenties. who's on the threshold of a whole new career. There was a picture of Damian in my newspaper.

Damian's wearing a sash across his torso in the photograph.

The sash reads: "Miss Wintersun."

A man has won the Miss Wintersun Beauty Contest in Australia.

"Now that I've done this who knows what I can do?" said a teary Damian. "I don't want to cause any waves with *Miss Australia*, but I'm going for it."

Sure, go for it, Damian. It's just one more skirmish in the never-ending Battle of the Sexes. Nobody's ever figured that one out, but the late comedian George Burns came as close as anybody I know.

"There will always be a battle between the sexes," said George, "because men and women want different things.

"Men want women and women want men."

Idling with the Filthy Rich

Legend has it that F. Scott Fitzgerald once sniffed to Hemingway, "The rich . . . are not as we are." To which Hemingway is supposed to have grumped, "No. They have more money."

Cute story. Too cute, actually.

The truth is, the rich have a lot of perks beyond mere filthy lucre to grease their glide through this vale of tears. For instance, the rich of New York City have . . . well, for starters they have Mister Newspaperman, an independent home delivery specialist who operates on the posh Upper East Side of Manhattan. Mister Newspaperman basically fetches the dailies for affluent New Yorkers who wouldn't want to sully their pinkies with the common folk at a newsstand. But he also offers a unique service for those of his clients with specialized tastes. If his customers are too embarrassed to admit that they like reading the racy tabloid, the *New York Post*, Mister Newspaperman is more than pleased to deliver the *Post* to their door, tastefully folded inside a copy of the *New York Times*.

Here in Canada, a somewhat similar service was performed until recently for the landed gentry of Forest Hill and Rosedale, two bejewelled hamlets within the city of Toronto. Only in that case the garbage was taken away, rather than delivered. The City of Toronto provided free side and rear entrance garbage pickup for some six thousand of the tonier chateaus of Rosedale and Forest Hill. That's right — the sanitation navvies shuffled right up to the house and wrestled those cans from doorstep to disposal truck at no extra charge.

Well, no extra charge to the plutocrats who lived there. The Toronto taxpaying rabble used to shell out about $365,000 a year to keep the service humming along. No longer, though. Toronto City Council "reviewed" the two-tier garbage system. Rosedalers and Forest Hillians now have to rely on their own servant staff to ferry the garbage from below stairs to curbside.

Still pretty small potatoes in the pavilion of Wretched Excess, however. Doesn't hold a candle to the 5,400 shoes of Imelda Marcos or Jimmy and Tammy Faye Bakkers' air-conditioned dog houses. Can't touch Liberace's rhinestone-studded Steinway or Aristotle Onassis's whale-foreskin-covered bar stools.

Ah, but to see true crassness, you have to go back . . . way back. To the time of Louis XV . . . The Sun King, who wore a long coat entirely covered with diamonds. A coat that in the late seventeenth century was worth 14 million francs.

Or back still further. To the time of the Roman Empire and the reign of Emperor Heliogabalus, circa 200 A.D. Now there's a guy who really knew how to spend money. Heliogabalus covered the usual Roman debaucheries — banquets where guests feasted on nightingale tongues, orgies where guests rutted with anything that moved . . . but his Wretched Excess Pièce de Résistance would have to be the time he ordered his slaves to bring him ten thousand pounds of . . . cobwebs.

History doesn't record what Heliogabalus did with his five tons of cobwebs, but they do tell us that the emperor met a fittingly Imperial end. He was hacked to death, Julius Caesar style, by his own Praetorian Guard.

Not all rich folks are spenders, of course. Take the First Baron Rothschild who lived and thrived from 1840 to 1915. Story goes that one evening the Baron popped out of a hansom cab and tossed the driver a coin. "'Ere!" piped the driver. "Your Lordship's son always gives me a good deal more than this."

"I daresay he does," replied the Baron, "but then, he has a rich father."

Bewitched, Bothered, and Bewhiskered

Here's a distressing dollop of news: according to an Angus Reid poll, a whopping 74 percent of Canadian women prefer their men to be face naked. Only 26 percent — a measly quarter — prefer to snuggle up to someone with fur on his chin.

Distressing. Well, distressing if you happen to have fur on your face as I do. My beard was my Centennial Project. Started growing it back in '67 to bring real meaning to the phrase, "letting it all hang out." Well, I was living in a Madrid flophouse with no hot water at the time so it wasn't what you'd call a real sacrifice.

In all the years since then, I've only been beardless once. Got involved in a Radio Gabathon to raise money for the Thunder Bay Symphony Orchestra. I must've been into the Kakabeka Cream Lager that evening, because I promised to shave off my beard if donations went over the $35,000 mark. The phones lit up, the TBSO cleaned up, and I got shaved. No one in Thunder Bay, including my young daughter, had ever seen me without a beard.

To a rousing a capella chorus of "Ewwwwwwww, put it back!" — I retired from public view for a couple of weeks, regrew my chin whiskers, and have never let Victor Kiman or the Brothers Gillette near my throat since.

But it's a lonely, thankless lifestyle choice. Aside from the fact that three-quarters of Canadian womenfolk treat you like a middle-aged Wolfman, possibly rabid, there are the jokes and epithets. You get called "Beardo" and "Fuzzface." Family comedians put cans of flea powder in your Christmas stocking. They ask you if the swallows go south in the fall or stay under your chin year-round. And you get the Fred Allen joke at least once a year: "Say, boy, you look like you swallowed a St. Bernard and left the tail hanging out, har, har!"

Have you noticed you don't see many beards in the Reform Party? A lot of Christian fundamentalists are really down on beards. Kind of odd, considering who they worship, but the Lord works in mysterious ways, I guess.

Allan Sherman, the sixties "Hello Muddah . . ." comedian, used to have a beard and one day he was confronted by a Bible thumper who snapped, "That beard is disgusting. Why did you decide to grow it?"

I'll always treasure Allan Sherman's reply. "But madam, I didn't," he said. "I never decided to grow a beard. When I was twelve years old, God decided I should have a beard, and the next morning there it was on my face — but I took a razor and cut it off. Next morning, God put it back, but I cut it off again. We went on like that day after day — God putting the beard on my face every night and me cutting it off every morning. After thirty-eight years of this, I finally decided to let God have his way."

Which reminds me of the story of another great beard. The one attached to George Bernard Shaw's mug. Shaw once explained how he came to wear a beard — because of a conversation with his father. "I was about five at the time," said Shaw, "and I was standing at my father's knee whilst he was shaving. I said to him, 'Daddy, why do you shave?'

"He looked at me in silence, for a full minute, then answered, 'Why the hell do I?' and threw the razor out the window. He never did again."

Ah, Allan Sherman, Mister Shaw Senior, George Bernard Shaw, Robertson Davies, Santa Claus. Me. Bearded guys. Just slightly ahead of our time. Wake up, ladies.

Too Dumb To Be Crooked

Is it a bigger crime to rob a bank or to open one?

A chap by the name of Ted Allen wrote the above. I think Mister Allen had his thumb squarely on one of the elusive characteristics of crime: its chameleon-like ability to pass itself off as something else.

When you think about it, it's really rather remarkable that so many people take up a life of crime, considering there are so many legal ways to be dishonest. We live in a time when political bumboys who have weaseled their way into a Senate appointment cynically vote themselves a massive pay raise smack in the face of a recession-ravaged populace. We live in a time when a roundly reviled departing prime minister casually attempted to sell his used furniture back to the very people who paid for it in the first place.

If you can get away with scams like that legally — who needs to break the law?

Still, break the law we do. Some of us, at any rate. And it is the inept and ham-handed ways in which we break the law that offer, if nothing more, some comic relief for the rest of the Great Unwashed that continue to plod the Straight and Narrow.

Take, for instance, the case of Eugene "Butch" Flenough, Jr., of Austin, Texas. Eugene, down to his last five bucks, decided to knock over a pizza joint late one evening. Cleverly enough, Eugene reasoned that since there were several members of the staff still on the premises, it might be a good idea to conceal his identity. Accordingly, he donned his motorcycle helmet, complete with tinted visor, burst through the door, ordered everybody up against the wall, cleaned out the till, and fled.

Imagine Eugene's surprise when the Texas Rangers were practically at his door to greet him when he got home. The Rangers told him he had been positively identified by several staff members. Impossible, thought Eugene "Butch" Flenough, Jr. How could anyone identify me when I was wearing my motorcycle helmet with the tinted visor?

And so he was — the one with "Eugene 'Butch' Flenough, Jr." neatly stencilled across the front.

Eugene was plain dumb. Daniel Wakefield was Dumb Squared. Wakefield walked into a bank in Pretoria, South Africa, last year with a gun in one hand and a canvas bag in the other.

He was wearing a mask — which, cleverly enough, did not have his name stencilled on it. Wakefield threw the bag at a teller, and told her to fill it with folding money. She did. Wakefield fled. So far, so good — for Wakefield at any rate.

But fifty minutes later, a bare-faced Dan Wakefield shows up in the same bank. "He was still wearing the same clothes and carrying the same bag," testified one of the tellers. "We all recognized him the minute he walked in and we called the police."

By the time Wakefield arrived at the teller's wicket, detectives were sidling up to him from every quarter of the compass. Blithely, Wakefield emptied the $4,212 he'd stolen on the counter and chirped, "I'd like to open an account."

Say goodnight, Mister Wakefield.

Dumb — but not dumb enough to hold a dunce cap to William Saunders of New York. A couple of years ago, Saunders stormed into an office of AT&T in Manhattan, armed to the teeth and threatening mayhem. He took fourteen hostages. Police cordoned off the building. SWAT units slipped into position on rootftops and in adjacent offices.

Fortunately, thirteen of the hostages managed to escape on their own. How? They asked Saunders — one at a time — for permission to go and get a drink of water. They never returned. Saunders eventually surrendered to police.

How come I never get to play poker with guys like William Saunders?

People lament about the rise in crime. I say, "Thank the Gods for Dumb Crooks." Imagine the shape we'd be in if they were as wily as our politicians.

2

Symbols, Icons, Emblems, and Fads

Don't Look Now,
But . . .

I suppose Homo sapiens is the only back-patting species this old planet ever produced. We're great at self-congratulation. We never tire of accepting kudos for our magnificent accomplishments — be they snapshots of Saturn or laser surgery on a fullback's knee. We're so busy taking bows and murmuring, "Thank you . . . it was nothing . . . ," that I fear sometimes we overlook the truly fabulous contributions of mankind. The innovations that have transformed ALL of our lives, be we prince or putz. Ladies and gentlemen, could we have a great big hand for . . .

The zipper.

Well, sure, the zipper! Can you imagine life without it? We've got zippers on our windbreakers; zippers on our sleeping bags; zippers on our skirts and purses; zippers on our parkas and tent flaps.

And, of course, men have zippers front and just south of centre, where we need them most.

'Twas not always thus. As a matter of fact, it was not thus for about the first six thousand years of recorded history. Mankind started keeping a diary in 4241 B.C. — and as we can see, for the next six millennia, every time a guy got into his pants in the morning, he either tied, pinned, pegged, snapped, buttoned, laced, trussed, or held them up with his spare hand . . . but he did not zip.

We had no such option until 1893, when a Chicago tinkerer by the name of Whitcomb Judson got a patent for what he called his "clasp locker."

It wasn't anything you'd care to zip yourself into. Judson's clasp locker consisted of two strips of wicked-looking hook-and-eye fasteners that theoretically meshed when you pulled the tab up. Judson's invention was Gothic and ungainly and looked like it could do you serious damage.

A zipperless world did not beat a path to Judson's laboratory door. But other engineers were intrigued and played around with the idea. Twenty years later, a lighter and more reliable refinement on the Judson fastener was created, and the modern zipper was born.

It still wasn't much good. The first zippers were made of cheap soft metal that rusted faster than a Trabant in a Toronto winter. Back then, zippers had to be unstitched from a garment before it was washed, then painstakingly sewed back in place before the garment was ironed.

Tailors, seamstresses, housewives, and bachelor schoolteachers maintained a glacial demeanour towards the device.

That was back in the early 1900s, but even I, a relative pup, can remember when pants zippers were not the smooth and virtually fail-safe gizmos we take for granted today. I can recall when zippers routinely jammed or derailed completely while only halfway to their destination, leaving the pant wearer with a uselessly dangling tab pull and a serious social problem.

Of course, with a potentially embarrassing situation like that, it's all in how you handle it. There is the story of Sir Winston Churchill appearing in the House of Commons with his fly at half-mast. On being discreetly informed that his, ah, dress was in need of adjustment, the British Bulldog, then eighty-six years old, harpooned his informant with a baleful glare and growled, "Dead birds don't fall out of nests."

When you can come up with retorts like that, who cares whether your zipper works?

Holidays for the Politically Correct

Don't look now, folks, but trick-or-treating could be just a little trickier this year. Political correctness has come to Halloween. Yessir . . . the Language Police have cordoned off the centuries-old festivity and declared it ripe for sanitizing. According to a group called the Equity-Affirmative Advisory Committee, there are some costumes your children should not dress up in because said costumes could cause "unpleasant and/or hurtful situations."

So what should your kids *not* dress up as this year? Here's the list: Gypsy. Native Indian. East Indian. Elderly Person. Disabled Person. Slave. Witch. Hobo. Devil.

I see. Yes, fine. Well that leaves, ahh . . . pretty well nothing, actually. I guess the kids could still dress up as the Maytag Repair Man or a fire hydrant or a largish root vegetable, but I can't see a lot of enthusiasm for those options. Maybe we should just keep the kids indoors on Halloween singing rounds of Solidarity Forever.

Call me old-fashioned, but I find it hard to imagine a Halloween without clutches of pint-sized devils and witches and hoboes and goblins skittering across my front porch, Unicef boxes in hand. What is it exactly that we're protecting them from?

Well, everything it seems. Even criticism by their peers. There's a principal of a public school down in Weymouth, Massachusetts, who's made the ultimate affirmative action proposal to his school board. Mandatory clapping. John Dowling, principal of East Intermediate Secondary School, wants to make it compulsory for audiences to clap at the end of all auditorium performances — good, fair, or dismal.

"If you get a ten-year-old girl who's singing her heart out, we'd like to see the children clapping, whether she's good or not." And he adds,

45

"We have written standards for other types of behaviour, so why not the same for auditorium behaviour?"

Oh, brave, new, automatically affirming world! Why even put the dear wee ones through the trauma of performance? Why not just a continuous tape loop of thunderous applause broadcast over the public address system from roll call to lights out?

Sure. And once we've exorcised the evils of Halloween, let's go after the real festive sacrilege. Christmas and its chief agent — Santa Claus.

Who is this overweight, conspicuously costumed, nocturnal, breaking-and-entering alien with no visible means of support? Does he collect GST on all the gifts he leaves? Does he declare to Revenue Canada all the milk and cookies he scarfs? Are the elves getting time and a half? Does the SPCA know about the work burden those reindeer face? Does he have a licence for that off-road vehicle, which, by the way, appears to have no running lights for night travel . . .

I'd like to put these questions to the infamous Mister Claus. Preferably in a court of law. The Supreme Court, even. Provided we could have the Chief Justice dress up as Ronald McDonald and the court officers all wearing Barney costumes.

I mean . . . we wouldn't want to frighten the children, would we?

Miracle Inventions
That Never Were

Not too many years ago, a British writer by the name of Sacheverell Sitwell looked out at the welter of wires and tubes and silicon chips burgeoning about him and blurted, "Have there not been enough inventions?"

Well, you can see the man's point. We have satellite discs and cars that talk back to us, Stealth bombers and silicone breast implants, bathing suits that block out lechers' eyes, but not sun's rays, super glue stronger than steel, and fishing rods that bend double at the strike of a goldfish — enough already, right?

Wrong. The simple answer is we never needed a new invention more. An invention such as — well, how about something that would solve our balance of payments crisis, eliminate exhaust emission pollution, and give a breather to declining fossil fuel stock all at one swat? How about a source of cheap, abundant, non-polluting energy? Joseph Warren has it in a suitcase by his workbench, but nobody wants to know.

Or so Joseph Warren claims. Joe's a retiree in his eighties who lives in Kitchener, Ontario, and spends his days cranking out letters and press releases to governments and reporters extolling the virtues of his Pendynamics Electric Power Appliance. It's a device, Joe says, that, mass-produced, would be roughly the size of a fridge, cost about half the price of a car, and would provide all the power a family could use for nothing.

What a wonderful invention. Too bad we've been here before. Remember Guido Franch? He's the guy who many years ago announced the discovery of Mota Fuel. That's atom, spelled backwards. Guido's miracle invention was a green pill, which, when dropped in water, converted it to high octane gasoline at a cost of pennies per gallon. Unlike Joseph Warren, who refuses to demonstrate his invention, Guido was happy to show reporters his green pill in action right in his own backyard by firing up his lawnmower with the stuff. Or at least he was until one reporter caught him red — make that green — handed, palming a flask of aviation fuel into the Toro gas tank. You didn't hear much from Guido after that.

Then there was Joseph Newman of Mississippi who tried to patent his so-called energy output machine. Mister Newman really went out on a Newtonian limb. He said his machine *produced* more power than it *consumed.* The U.S. Patent Office found that, in fact, it produced something between 45 and 60 percent as much energy as it gobbled, which in terms of efficiency placed it somewhere between a used car and a teenage couch potato. Joseph Newman cried conspiracy, charging that the U.S. Patent Office was in cahoots with the big oil companies to keep cheap energy off the market. Joseph Warren of Kitchener refuses to patent his Pendynamic appliance for fear his idea will be stolen. Always seems to happen with miracle fuel inventions.

Well, at least we can applaud a real inventor by the name of Cork Foster, of St. Thomas, Ontario. Cork runs a mail-order business and, like a lot of us, worries about environmental abuse. Such as those horrible nondegradable styrofoam chips he uses to protect shipped merchandise.

Used to use. Cork Foster has come up with a replacement. Which is why when you get something from Cork Foster's mail-order firm, chances are it will come packed in . . . popcorn. A quarter of the cost and nothing in the garbage can. Packaging that can be recycled with just a little salt and butter. Now that's an invention.

Please Fence Me In

Something there is that doesn't love a wall.
That sends the frozen ground-swell under it.
                                    ROBERT FROST

I do a lot of country walking, and one of the great pleasures of my rambles comes when I stumble across a stone wall, those architectural artifacts of settlers long dead. They wind along the crests of hills and undulate through groves of poplar and cedar like lumpy Gothic serpents, separating ancient, overgrown pastures from the remnants of once-fruitful apple orchards. More often than not, the farmhouses that sheltered the people who built the walls have fallen to ruin — disappeared even, swallowed up by brush and bramble and burdock.

But the walls live on, though they're often tumbledown and gap-toothed, reduced to playing host to lichens and rodents and skinny, stubborn maple and walnut saplings. Robert Frost was right — something there is that doesn't love a wall — and that something is an implacable landlady by the name of Mother Nature.

Hardly anyone builds stone walls in my part of the country anymore. Post and wire, steel mesh, and, of course, the electrified barbed wire fence are all much easier and more cost-effective.

And utterly graceless.

The old stone walls are a marvel to behold. There's not a gobbet of mortar or a lick of cement to hold them together. No diploma-dripping engineer has a hand in their construction, and yet there they are, still standing, still, more or less, doing their job: separating this from that — forty, fifty, even a hundred years later.

Or, in some cases, thousands of years later. I'm told that there are still stone walls running across the fields of Cornwall in England that were built by the rough, red hands of ancient Britons, back in the time of the Caesars.

The stone walls on this side of the Atlantic are somewhat younger, but no less magnificent.

Extensive, too. I have no idea how many miles of stone walls you could find if you measured the rocky remnants from Joe Batt's Arm to overgrown homesteads on Vancouver Island, but I do know there's a U.S. Agriculture Department census from 1871 that indicates some 252,000 miles of stone wall in New York and New England alone. And that was 120 years ago.

You still don't have to walk too far in most of rural settled Canada before you stub your hiking boot on the leftovers of somebody's back-wrenching labour, generations past.

Do I over-romanticize these granite and limestone mementoes of pioneer days? Perhaps. A geologist at the University of Connecticut says those old stone walls are not all that noble. According to Robert Thorson, they aren't even fences, primarily. What they are, says the professor, is pioneer garbage dumps. "Linear landfills," to use his phrase.

Professor Thorson says those old stone walls merely represent the first man-made upheaval of the environment. The opening salvo in a massive deforestation offensive.

Well, I suppose farmers clearing land in order to grow crops and raise cattle could be viewed as environmental assaulters.

But you have to wonder whether Professor Thorson ever speculates about where his bread and potatoes come from.

For my part, I believe I will continue to walk in the woods and look for those old handmade, man-made walls. And when I find one, I plan to park my bum on it, and run my hands across it, and think a few kind thoughts about the men and women who paid in sweat and aching muscles to put it there.

They may be ghosts now, but they're still my neighbours.

And as Robert Frost observed: good fences make good neighbours.

Scribbling for Eternity

Got a bit of a botanical blast from the past while walking through the bush a while back. Came to a big old beech tree that must be at least a hundred years old. It's been there since I was a kid, for sure. I know that. Because it carries my signature. Right down about spare tire level you can just make out an inscription inside a scabby heart that reads A.B. and M.J.C.

The M.J.C. is none of your business, but about the A.B. I cannot tell a lie. I carved that there with my trusty Boy Scout knife — must be forty years ago, at least.

My contribution to the world stock of freelance graffiti.

I didn't know it at the time, but I was carrying on an ancient and venerable tradition. Humans have been scribbling names and ads and slogans on trees and walls and rocks for centuries. Millennia, in fact. There are Greek graffiti chiselled into the rocks near the ancient Egyptian town of Abu Simbel that go back to the sixth century B.C.

Timeless poetry perhaps? Wisdom of the ages? Nope. Archeologists report that most of it is the prehistorical equivalent of the same dumb stuff graffitophiles scribble in the twentieth century.

Sort of . . . Thucydides was here.

That's the most common kind of graffiti — an attempt by some anonymous scribe to let the rest of the world know he or she is alive. Kilroy Was Here. John Loves Mary. A.B. and M.J.C.

Then there's slogan graffiti. One of the oldest came to light when archeologists excavated the city of Pompeii, buried by an eruption of Mount Vesuvius in 79 A.D. On one of the walls is a handwritten notice you can still read that says in Latin: "The United Fruitmen with Helvius Vestalis urge you to elect Marcus Holconius . . ."

Occasionally graffiti transcend themselves and instead of a one-shot advertisement they become a kind of dialogue, where one graffitist comments on the work of another.

Thus the cryptic call-and-response recorded on a Harvard washroom wall a few years back. "GOD IS DEAD: NIETZSCHE," one scribbler wrote. And underneath that, in another hand: "NIETZSCHE IS DEAD: GOD."

Another washroom wall featured the lament: "MY MOTHER MADE ME A HOMOSEXUAL." Beneath that, someone else wrote, "IF I SENT HER THE WOOL, WOULD SHE MAKE ME ONE?"

And this triple-barreled salvo, which is probably too good to be true: "TO DO IS TO BE: DESCARTES."

Under that: "TO BE IS TO DO: SARTRE."

And one line lower: "DO BE DO BE DO: SINATRA."

Most popular graffito of all time? Probably the one I mentioned earlier — "Kilroy Was Here." For reasons nobody seems quite able to explain, that slogan suddenly started appearing everywhere during World War II.

Nobody ever found out who Kilroy was, but it's taken for granted he was an American. Mind you, there was a Canadian wartime Kilroy equivalent. His name was Clem. And no one knew who he was either, but the phrase "Clem Was Here" showed up regularly in the damnedest places, especially on armed forces property. In fact, one army base commander got so exasperated with the elusive Clem that he called a snap inspection one day and blistered the ears of the whole camp while they stood at attention. Told them in a fury of oaths and imprecations that he did not EVER want to see the phrase "Clem Was Here" again, anywhere on the base, then dismissed the company.

After which the C.O. returned to his office, looked down at his blotter, and saw a pencilled scrawl that read: "Wot! No Clem!"

Ah, Clem — where are you when we need you?

Reel Life

There's an old story from the earliest days of movies about a turn-of-the-century British actor who sailed magisterially under the magnificent moniker of Sir Herbert Beerbohm Tree. Sir Herbert was a Shakespearean actor, vintage variety. He trod the boards and belted it out from the guts, without benefit of stage directors, hidden mikes, or teleprompters. When the filmmaker D. W. Griffith cast the actor in the title role of a silent film version of Macbeth, Sir Herbert showed up on the movie set, cleared his throat, glared about him for a few seconds, then thundered, "Take that black box away; I cannot act in front of it."

He was talking about the movie camera — a new-fangled intrusion in his time. Nowadays, when people tell that story they do it in a bemused and patronizing tone. Poor, old, hopelessly out of sync Sir Herbert. Confounded by a camera. What a gormless Luddite.

Well I don't think so. I think Sir Herbert was prophetic. Just like the early Indians who hated cameras and refused to pose for frontier photographers. They had a message for us and we weren't listening. I think they were trying to warn us about the video camera.

Too late now, of course. Video cameras are everywhere. And they're getting cheaper and lighter and tinier with every edition of the Radio Shack catalogue.

They've changed the way we live. People don't go to see Niagara Falls or Gros Morne National Park or the Calgary Stampede anymore — they go to film them.

Not that these people are embryonic D. W. Griffithses or anything, you understand. They just have these dandy new cameras and an appositional thumb, and thought the world could use eight hundred overexposed yards of Marge and the kids grinning moronically in front of Chateau Lake Louise.

Just think of the thousands and thousands of curling miles of ineffably boring home video footage we're spawning year after year. If Satan has a postmodernist fibre in his being, he's undoubtedly redesigning Hades as I speak. To hell with sulphur and brimstone and pitchforks. A truly eternal inferno would be a huge, dark rec room where the damned are sentenced to watch everybody else's home movies. Forever.

Which reminds me of the most ominous video tale I know. It's a news story about a wedding in Torquay, England. Claire Lockett was the bride, but her mother Rita was the clucking Momma Hen. Rita oversaw everything. The two hundred guests, the five-star hotel, the orchestra, the food, the decorations. And the video. It was all Rita Lockett's baby — to the tune of £18,000.

The wedding was glorious. But the wedding video was dreadful. The cameraman was an amateur. He missed the bride going up the aisle. He didn't cover the reception at all. Rita Lockett was expecting *Gone with the Wind*. She got an Industrial Short.

You've already guessed what Rita Lockett is going to do about it, right? That's right. She is restaging the wedding. The hotel is rebooked, the orchestra is tuned up once more, the flowers and food have been reordered, and all the guests have been reinvited — and asked to wear the same clothes. Rita Lockett is bringing in an out-of-town professional video recording firm to record it properly.

Life is being replayed for the sake of the video.

Reality as a rerun.

I'm not sure what it means, but I am not going to rent a tux.

I intend to wait for the novel.

Fabrics — Fabulous and Otherwise

Can you remember wool?

Do you go as far back as cotton and flannel and silk?

Are you antique enough to remember REAL fibres manufactured by actual flesh-and-blood sheep and mandible-to-the-grindstone silkworms and sturdy, upright cotton plants photosynthesizing like troopers, row on downy-headed row?

Yesterday's threads, I'm afraid. Irish linens, Harris Tweeds, and Egyptian cotton are as out of date as brass cuspidors and whalebone corsets. Now our clothes are more likely to trace their pedigree to a row of test tubes or some obscure Erlenmeyer flask in a chemical research lab. Today's clothes spring from plastics — weird and soulless polymers with Star Trekkish monikers like Lycra, Neoprene, Fibranne, and Polypropylene.

It all goes back to a fateful day in the 1870s, when a New England manufacturer of billiard balls offered a $10,000 prize to anyone who could come up with a cheaper substitute for his increasingly expensive ivory imports. A young printer from Albany, New York, won the money with a flexible, transparent substance that he called "celluloid."

In biblical fashion, celluloid begat Bakelite, which begat cellophane, which begat acetate, which begat . . . well, suffice to say that by the Dirty Thirties, the developed world was awash in vinyl, Plexiglas, Melmac, styrene, Formica, and polyester.

Then, in 1940 the Dupont Chemical Company announced the development of yet another new plastic "passing in strength and elasticity any previously known textile fibres." In fact, early claims promised that a pair of women's stockings made from this "magical synthetic" would "last forever."

The new plastic was nylon and predictions of its immortality were somewhat optimistic. But it was still a smash hit when it landed on the notions counters of New York department stores on May 15, 1940. Dupont researchers allotted 72,000 pairs for the test marketing. Sales were limited to two pairs per customer.

They sold out in eight hours.

The nylon stockings should have been an utter failure. They developed ladders and runs and rips and tears faster than cobwebs in a hurricane.

But women loved them. They lined up to buy them faster than Dupont could turn them out.

That opened the floodgates for plastics manufacturers. For the first time in 100,000 years, man wasn't taking nature's raw material — rock, wood, and animal fibre — and turning it into something serviceable. For the first time he was "playing God" — taking long chains of molecules and bending them to his will.

Which begat whole new textile mutants. Banlon. Orlon. Viyella.

And rayon.

Rayon is my nomination for the Synthetic From Hell. Rayon shirts for men came out in the fifties. The big selling point was you could wear a rayon shirt all day long, wash it out in a motel sink at night, and in the morning — presto — ready to wear.

Which was true, I guess. But there was a penalty. In the winter, a rayon shirt was so cold it welded to your nipples. In the summer, to wear a rayon shirt was to have your own portable sauna.

And the smell. Phew! Without getting too graphic, let's just say that the odours rayon coaxed from the human armpit were such that you pretty well HAD to wash those shirts out in the motel sinks every evening. Lunchtimes too, if possible.

Not that the revulsion of rayon detracted from the popularity of synthetics. People still lined up to buy the stuff. Which is why today we have such mutations as Lyocell, Ultrasuede, viscose, and my favourite — Spandex.

Spandex. That's the elasticized, second-skin garment that looks like it came out of a spray can. You see Olympic gymnasts and bicycle couriers wearing it. Which would be fine if they were the *only* folks who donned Spandex, but inevitably you see it on folks who have no business wearing anything that outlines their figure. In Spandex they look like a sackful of bowling balls.

Not that I'm making fun of them. Hey — me? Make fun of fat? That's me over there in the shadows.

Wearing the tweed muumuu.

Can It Make You Thinner? Of Corset Can

It is one of the enduring ironies of the late twentieth century that while perhaps you and certainly I and definitely Roseanne Barr strive desperately to lose a few pounds, most of the people in the world are scrambling just as desperately to gain a couple.

The grim spectre of starvation stalks the Third World, but here in Fat Cat Central we swirl our wine spritzers and nibble on carrot sticks while we moan about how tough it is to take off weight.

There are more ways to reduce than there are calories in a banana split. There's a new diet every week.

And then there's exercise — anything from bare-knuckle mountaineering to low-impact aerobics. The more crazed among the Gravitationally Challenged resort to surgery — lyposuction to hoover away those rolls of fat; not to mention "tummy tucks," which short-circuit the alimentary canal. Some folks have their jawbones wired shut to prevent the intake of solids.

Simple, medically supervised fasting would do the trick for most of us, except that's a little too much like . . . well, the sort of thing that goes on in icky places like Somalia, Ethiopia, and Bangladesh.

At the risk of being dismissed as just another Phoney Baloney Svelteness Guru, I'd like to tell you about a way to look thinner that works faster than any diet plan or exercise regime you ever heard of.

What's more, it's a method with a proven track record. Our overweight ancestors were using this trick to look slim centuries ago.

It's called the corset.

The corset actually dates back to at least the early sixteenth century — and the first ones were probably worn for therapeutic reasons, rather than vanity. It didn't take long however, for people to realize that the average human body looked a lot trimmer when it was lashed into a straightjacket of whalebones and cloth than it did when it was allowed to droop and bulge naturally. By the late seventeenth and early eighteenth century, just about everybody in England who could afford a corset was sitting or standing unusually erect and breathing in shallow little gasps. The corset was the chosen instrument of torture for all who would be chic.

"Torture" is no exaggeration. Girls as young as thirteen were trussed up in corsets in order that their figures be "improved." And the corsets got tighter and tighter. During the 1700s, fashionable corsets literally drove the female waistline down. Not to mention "in." Some girls had their waistlines reduced by a mind-boggling eight inches.

As time went on, common sense seemed to retreat. The 1800s saw the dawn of the "hourglass" figure. The eighteen-inch waist became the ideal. Ladies of fashion even went as far as having their lower ribs surgically removed to accommodate a snugger corset and a waspier waist.

The ultimate corset absurdity arrived with the not-so Gay Nineties and a revolutionary corset engineered with a complexity worthy of Michelangelo.

Or perhaps the Marquis de Sade. This construction featured a minuscule waist and a rigid front, so that the woman's breasts were pushed forward while her hips were forced to the rear.

If X rays had been available they would have revealed an anatomical obscenity — women's spines torqued and twisted until they looked like large capital Ss — all in the name of fashion.

The popularity of corsets died out, thank heaven, about 1910 and they haven't been a serious fashion threat since.

Could they make a comeback? Hey, in a society that endorses silicone breast implants, face lifts, and stiletto high heels, anything is possible, I suppose . . . but a garment as stupid and health-threatening as the corset?

Personally, I wouldn't hold my breath.

Fluttering the Lawn

If, like me, you find yourself on your front lawn some sweaty, sultry summer Saturday afternoon, desperately wanting to blame somebody . . . you can blame Edwin Budding. Edwin Budding was the foreman at a textile plant in Gloucestershire back in the early 1800s, and the world would be a better, quieter place if Edwin Budding had just tended to his warps and wefts there, but no — Edwin had to get curious. Edwin had to figure out how he could take the rotary shearing machine used to cut the nap off cotton in the factory, and adapt it to . . . outside work.

Within a few years, Edwin Budding had it figured out, and he applied for a patent. His new device was intended for "cropping or shearing the vegetable surface of lawns, grass-plots or pleasure compounds."

It was 1830 and Edwin Budding had given the world its first mechanical lawn mower.

Edwin Budding, in his stunning naivete, advertised that "country gentlemen will find in using my machine an amusing, useful and healthful exercise."

Country gentlemen didn't. But a lot of country gentlemen's wives thought it was a smashing idea to have the grass trimmed brush-cut short on a regular basis, and for the next ninety years, country gentlemen, luckless teenagers, and anybody who could be coaxed, coerced, or sentenced to lawn duty sweated and heaved like canal horses behind clones and knock-offs of Edwin Budding's infernal invention.

And then, in 1919, a backyard breakthrough. Another Edwin — an American Army colonel by the name of Edwin George — invented the gasoline lawn mower! Did it revolutionize the sinister worldwide mania for giving haircuts to lawns? It certainly did. Lawns immediately became ten times larger and indentured lawn-mower navvies got to sweat and heave like canal horses while inhaling gasoline fumes.

Evolution continues. A scant seventy-odd years after Edwin George's ear-splitting refinement, along comes Thomas Noonan of Havertown, Pennsylvania. Mister Noonan has just received a patent for Mobot — the world's first robotic lawn mower. Mobot has its very own micro-processor, which stores the programmed cutting route and finds its way around by responding to sensors imbedded in the lawn.

And will the world leap at the chance to turn its backyards over to a roboclipper? I doubt it. Who needs yet another computer in their life to foul up? In fact, the lawn cutters among us seem to be heading in quite a different direction. It all has to do with the increased interest in aerobic workouts. Not to mention concern over pollution — both air and noise. Seems that people are lining up to buy push mowers in numbers not seen since the 1950s when power mowers became the rage.

You know push mowers — the ones that flutter instead of roar? The ones that don't gobble fossil fuels, decapitate lawn ornaments, or suffer from carburetor malfunctions?

The kind Edwin Budding invented to amuse country gentlemen nearly 170 years ago?

Ersatz Exercise

To quote the eminently quotable Yogi Berra: "A fella can learn a lot by just watching." I was doing some watching up in Muskoka recently. Ontario cottage country, that is — all wooded hills and jewel-like lakes and chuckling rivers. Actually, I wasn't watching, I was doing a speech at one of the swanky new hotel complexes that opened up there not long ago. I had a few hours to myself, so I wandered around, checking out the place.

That's when I saw the sign. "COMING SOON," it read, "A BRAND NEW INDOOR RUNNING TRACK!"

Indoor running track?

Here I was in some of the most beautiful country that Canada has to offer, several hundred thousand acres of unfenced, unpolluted real estate with clean air, panoramic vistas, and uncrowded roads where a galoot could jog himself to death if he cared to . . .

And they were advertising an *indoor* running track?

Why?

I brooded about it over a beer with a pal of mine in the pub later that night. "It's not too complicated, ya dummy," she said. "An indoor running track is whatcha use on those days when it's too rainy or too cold or too snowy to run outside."

I don't buy it.

Rain and snow and cold are just nature's way of telling you to pull the covers over your head and forget about exercise until the weather clears — if not longer.

Besides, the indoor running track makes a perverse kind of sense if you view it in the context of other bizarre exercise options of late.

How about treadmills? You know — where you put on your shorts and your nine-way self-inflating running shoes and a headband . . . and then you step onto a rubber roller and pass a sweaty half hour pretending that you're actually loping through the countryside.

Or what about exercise bikes? Is it not somewhat insane that fitness fanatics use these gizmos to cycle like dervishes in basements and rec rooms and exercise clubs — when they could just as easily jump on a real two-wheeler and cycle around the block?

What is it about ersatz exercise anyway? Department stores advertise rowing machines — diabolical contraptions consisting of pulleys and clamps and levers that you can strap yourself into and pretend you're rowing a boat.

Why not just go down to the boathouse, lay down your five buck deposit, and take out a *real* dory? It'll be a lot more fun than trying to row across your living-room floor.

Or how about the ultimate in whacky workouts — The Stairmaster? For several hundred dollars you can risk a hernia levering a machine into your home that recreated the act of . . . climbing stairs.

Do you have any idea how *easy* it is to climb stairs — for free? Hotels have staircases. So do malls and condos and office buildings and hospitals. Hell, most houses have stairs — who needs to buy a stair-climbing machine?

Actually, folks may have already figured this out. There's a brand-new exercise mecca down in Los Angeles. It's called the Fourth Street Steps. It's a 189-step staircase that leads from the beach to the rim of the Santa Monica Canyon and it's where all the hippiest of the hip LA fitness buffs line up to strut their stuff. One trip up and down the stairs is equal to running up and down the stairwell of a ten-storey building. Nowadays, the Fourth Street Steps are awash with spandex-clad, Evian water–bearing fitness freaks lumbering up and down and down and up the stairs smiling conspiratorially at one another.

Exercise. I stole my personal fitness philosophy from a chap by the name of Chauncey Depew. Old Chauncey said, "I get my exercise acting as a pallbearer to my friends who exercise."

Hot Dogs: A History

I don't mean to whine, but I face a lot of trials in my working day.

There's the first one in the morning, of course — hitting the deck. Lying there with the blankets up under my chin and my noggin burrowed into the pillow, I can quickly list eight or twelve reasons why getting up qualifies as an Extremely Inferior Idea.

Alas, rising is but the first of many tribulations. There is the cold blast of water that invariably precedes my shower. There is my wretched cat miaoooooooowing piteously as it threads itself between my ankles. He's saying, "Feed me, for God's sake — it's been hours since I ate those chicken bones in the garbage."

Other daily afflictions? Oh, my, yes. There is the scraping of the windshield; the monotony of the chrome and plastic conga commute of vehicles on the highway into town. There is the unpleasant thug who mans the security desk, there is the depressing realization that, yes, I'm fifteen minutes late as usual, and, yes, everyone else is on time, working hard, taking just a moment to glance at their watches as I hustle by.

The daily hassles. But none of them comes even close to the mortification I feel when I face the greatest daily hurdle of all.

It comes at the end of my working day, when I leave my office building and head for the parking lot. Be calm, I tell myself. Almost there. Just another few yards of sidewalk to freedom.

But no. He's there, blocking my path. He's always there, Gus is. Just Gus and his cart.

A hot dog cart.

He sells me a hot dog just about every working day. I don't need a hot dog. All those hot dogs are not good for me. I can't afford to buy hot dog after hot dog, day after day.

But I do. I can't resist.

I flat-out love hot dogs.

Which is odd, because I mostly don't like junk food. I don't buy chocolate bars or jelly beans. I've never seen the inside of a Taco Bell or an Arby's and I only go to McDonald's for the coffee or to use the washroom. (Great washrooms at McDonald's.)

Hot dogs — different story. But then, as junk food goes, the hot dog is practically venerable. Nobody knows exactly how long folks have been wedging wieners in buns and slathering them with mustard, but the name alone goes all the way back to 1906.

Hot dogs were already popular fare back then, but they weren't called hot dogs. They were tagged everything from frankfurters to wieners and bread, bangers on a bun, tube steak sandwiches . . .

Even dachshund sausages.

At a New York Giants baseball game at the Polo Grounds in 1906, a newspaper cartoonist named Tad Dorgan sat in the stands watching the game and listening to the food vendors bellow, "Getcher red hot dachshund sausages!"

He thought about the vendors "barking" . . . he studied the dachshund-like swoop of the wiener in his hand . . . and something clicked in the cartoonist's brain. Dorgan whipped out a sketch pad and doodled a picture of a real dachshund dog, sandwiched in a bun and covered with mustard. Back at the office, Dorgan touched up the cartoon, then tried to come up with a caption.

He wanted the caption to read: "GET YOUR RED HOT DACHS-HUND SAUSAGES!" — but he wasn't sure how to spell "dachshund."

With his deadline looming, Dorgan thought, "Ah, what's the difference?" and he printed "GET YOUR HOT DOGS!"

— and created one of the most popular phrases of the century.

Hot dogs show up in songs and on ski slopes; in centre field and everyday conversation.

Win the lottery? One of the things you could yell is "Hot Dog!" Remember the Perry Como hit that goes "Hot Diggity, Dog Diggity, Boom What You Do To Me"? Kids who do somersaults on skis are called Hot Doggers. Pro baseball abounds with millionaire Hot Doggers.

And I'm not the only one who's addicted. Nearly 17 billion hot dogs are turned out each year. I'm not eating all of them.

Actually, I can't hold a napkin to a New Yorker who captured the world record by scarfing seventeen hot dogs in twelve minutes.

Think he'll ever look at another hot dog?

Sure he will. With relish.

Being of Sound Mind . . .

Will: n. a device for splitting heirs.

Ah, the Last Will and Testament. Was there ever a legal proceeding that caused more friction, fright, and fractiousness?

Okay, not counting marriage.

There have been some wild and woolly wills written ever since — well, I like to imagine that it goes back to the first primeval solicitor operating out of a storefront cave in prehistoric Mesopotamia. I see him as a smiling devil with meticulously combed eyebrows, wearing a three-piece pinstripe of mastodon worsted. I can visualize my Stone Age solicitor wedging a charred stick between the stiffening fingers of an expiring client, positioning the poor wretch in front of a stone tablet and urging him to "remember his friends" in writing.

And thus creating the first Last Will and Testament.

An awful lot of legal ink has flowed under the litigational bridge since those early days, but wills still make for some fascinating reading. Take the case of Henry, Earl of Stafford, an eighteenth-century English gentleman.

Well, not much of a gentleman, perhaps — but a plain speaker. Part of his will reads: "To the worst of women . . . unfortunately my wife, guilty as she is of all crimes, I leave five-and-forty brass halfpence which will buy a pullet for her supper."

Charles Dodgson, better known as Lewis Carroll, author of *Alice in Wonderland*, was more concerned with how people handled his send-off. "I request," wrote Dodgson, "that no Pall may be employed . . . Also that it may be a walking funeral . . . and generally that all details be simple and inexpensive, avoiding all things which are merely done for show."

The will of the great magician Houdini is more remarkable for what it did not contain. Contrary to hints he gave out while living, Houdini did not reveal his professional escape secrets in his will, but he did bequeath his collection of books on magic to the U.S. Library of Congress — and made sure that the rabbits he customarily pulled out of hats all found good homes with the children of his friends.

Silverdene Emblem O'Neill left a will at least as interesting as the name of the subject. "I have little in the way of material things to leave," says the will. "There is nothing of value I have to bequeath except my love and faith.

"These I leave to all those who loved me . . . Perhaps it is vain of me to boast when I am so near death, which returns all beasts and vanities to dust, but I have always been an extremely loveable dog."

That's right. Silverdene Emblem O'Neill ("Blemie" to his friends) was a dalmatian owned by the American playwright Eugene O'Neill, who also wrote up the will on his pet's behalf.

J. Edgar Hoover, the eccentric, if not downright kinky, head of the FBI for several hundred years, left the bulk of his estate to, not surprisingly, his "constant companion," Clyde Tolson.

There is no provision in the Hoover will for disposition of his fine collection of ballroom gowns.

Speaking of party girls, the late great Janis Joplin left a typically Joplinesque will to remember her by — money for an all-night party for two hundred pals at her favourite saloon in San Anselmo, California, "so all my friends can get blasted after I'm gone." For one night, all the Southern Comfort, tequila, vodka, and beer was on Janis.

Which brings us to the Last Will and Testament of Terry Oxley, recently deceased farmer near the town of Goole, in northeast England. From his hospital bed, Terry dictated the terms of his will, including a clause that instructs his solicitor to drop in to the nearby British Legion Pub in Goole once a week to pay George Carkwell's bar bill. George, you see is (was) Terry Oxley's drinking buddy. The Oxley Will states that George is to get "one thousand pints of bitter . . . on a basis of thirty-five pints a week."

Thirty-five pints a week, eh?

Well, cheers to you, Terry Oxley . . . and whichever bar you're bellying up to these days, be it celestial or infernal, I suggest you make room for your pal George.

At thirty-five pints a week, he should be alongside any day now.

Mexico: Getting the Bugs Out

I'd like to address one of the downsides of that Free Trade Agreement we've got with Mexico — nobody's talking about the influx of bugs we're going to have to get used to.

Oh yeah . . . Mexico's got a hard-backed beetle that we haven't seen in these parts for years. Once that agreement kicks in, there'll be no stopping them.

Personally, I can't say I mind. I kind of like the little critters. But I'll bet our car makers are quaking in their Guccis. Because the insect I'm talking about is the most famous beetle on four wheels. The Volkswagen beetle. The Bug.

The VW Bug was quite possibly the only good idea Adolph Hitler ever had. Back in 1933 he ordered engineers to design a simple, no frills automobile that could drive all day at sixty miles an hour and still be affordable for the average citizen. Two years later, the first Bug prototype was standing, hump backed, awaiting Hitler's approval. But by then Der Führer had other things to occupy what passed for his mind.

The Volkswagen Bug slipped into a thirteen-year limbo. Then, in 1948, Germans took the wraps off the prototype, dusted off the plans, and began production. One year later, the first Bug arrived in North America. Within a decade, more than 5 million had been sold.

For hordes of car-buying consumers, the Bug was love at first sight. Why? Because it was everything other cars were not. It was small, slow, and homely. It was also reliable and cheap.

Other cars promised to make you sexy, virile, respectable, flashy, and envied. The Bug just promised a cheap ride from A to B. Desotos and Buicks gave you space age dashboards with glowing dials. The Bug came with a wooden dipstick you could dunk in your tank to see how much gas was left.

Plus the Bug had a brilliant advertising campaign behind it. Remember the Volkswagen ads? "Think small." And the one that said, "After we paint the car, we paint the paint." And my favourite — the full-page ad that showed a Volkswagen Bug meandering through a trackless street in the middle of a blizzard, nothing else moving anywhere. The headline read: "Did you ever wonder how the snowplow driver gets to the snowplow?"

Such a good idea, the Volkswagen Bug — so why did it die? Well, put me down for paranoid if you like, but I don't think it did die. I think it was mercy-killed. What, a car that offered no frills and no expensive annual design changes? A car that was cheap to run and didn't break down much? A car people could keep for ten or fifteen years? Now how's a car tycoon gonna make any money out of that?

Whether it jumped or was pushed, the fact is Volkswagen stopped Bug production in Europe and in North America in the late seventies. But not before teaching some car makers an enduring lesson. You can see the Beetle smaller-is-better, plain and simple, legacy in many foreign cars. You can also read it in the red ink of Detroit's annual reports.

Today there's only one place in the world producing Volkswagen Beetles. It's a factory about seventy miles southeast of Mexico City. The assembly line there recently turned out the world's 21 millionth Bug.

I would guess that under the terms of the Free Trade Agreement, Volkswagen Bugs (albeit *hecho en* Mexico) might soon be on sale here in Canada. If I were in the new car market would I buy another Bug? If they're as good (and as relatively cheap) as the one I had back in the sixties — *absolutamente*.

And if I was a Canadian car maker, would I be worried about a Mexican bug infestation?

Si, Cisco.

Cool-As-a-Cucumber Cal

You know what this country needs, my friends? What this country needs is (I can't believe I'm saying this) another politician.

And an American politician at that.

Not just any American politician, mind. What this country could really use is the man who served as the thirtieth president of the United States of America, Calvin Coolidge. A pale, skinny Republican with red hair, freckles, a bony nose, a down-turned mouth that seldom turned up, and a pair of legs that almost certainly never did the Charleston.

As a warm and caring human being, Cool Cal fell somewhat short of, say, Alan Alda. Alice Roosevelt Longworth sniffed that Coolidge had been weaned on a pickle. His own wife claimed that he won her hand over other potential suitors only because "he outsat everybody else." Coolidge played his entire life like a bad poker hand, which is to say, close to the vest and stingily.

Most of all — and here's the blessed part about Calvin Coolidge — most of all, he hardly ever said a word. Well, he had a voice that quavered like a badly tuned A string on an open-fret banjo, but that's not the reason he bit his tongue. Coolidge didn't talk much because he knew it was smarter not to. "If you don't say anything, you won't be called on to repeat it," he once snapped — and for Cool Cal that was a filibuster.

His office efficiency amazed onlookers. Coolidge was able to see a near endless daisy chain of visitors and supplicants every day, but invariably finished his work at 5:00 p.m. A visiting governor moaned, "I'm at my desk every night until nine o'clock — what's the difference?" Coolidge looked at the governor and replied, "You talk back."

Coolidge got such a reputation as a zipperlip that it became a high-level Washington parlour game to get him to open up. One Washington socialite, famous for her beguiling ways, manoeuvred herself next to the president at a dinner and purred in his ear, "Mister Coolidge, I've made a bet that I can get more than two words out of you."

Cal swivelled in his seat and fixed the woman with a pair of iguana eyes. His lips parted . . . the voice croaked, "You lose."

But the man was not without humour and his spartan linguistics enhanced the effect. As in the time he and Mrs. Coolidge toured a government farm. When they came to the chicken pens, Mrs. Coolidge was quite taken with the rooster and inquired as to how many times he, um, you know, serviced the hens.

"Oh, dozens of times a day, ma'am," answered the tour guide.

"Tell that to the president," said Mrs. Coolidge.

The president came along and looked at the rooster. Informed of the animal's prowess, he asked, "Same hen every time?"

"Oh, no. Different hen each time, sir," said the guide.

"Tell that to Mrs. Coolidge," said Cal.

Good line, but I doubt that Cal was much fun in the sack. As Dorothy Parker said when informed that Coolidge had died, "How can they tell?"

Nope, Calvin Coolidge was probably a dud as a stud and certainly a disaster as a political leader.

But he was quiet about it. We've had a succession of disastrous politicians, randy and otherwise. I'd settle for quiet, wouldn't you?

A Non-Centsical Future

I can't remember precisely when I realized that life in Canada was going to Hell in a handcart. Somewhere between the gutting of passenger rail service . . . the cancellation of the Tommy Hunter Show . . . and the day the Air Canada flight attendants stopped handing out complimentary in-flight breath mints. Somewhere in that maelstrom of societal upheaval it occurred to me, "That's it. That's the end of civilization as we know it. Things really can't get much grimmer than this."

I was wrong. Things could get a lot grimmer. They just have. Ottawa is thinking about dropping the penny, so to speak.

The penny. The copper. The cent — as in one percentum of the dollar? Ottawa's thinking of getting rid of it.

Romantic tradition aside, it's hard to find fault with the idea. The penny is not what you'd call a big revenue maker. Quite the opposite. You know it actually costs Ottawa two cents for every penny it puts out? That's bad business, even by government standards.

The other weird thing about Canadian pennies is — once the government puts them out — they disappear. Canadians don't keep pennies in circulation. They hoard them as if they were emeralds or rubies. There are more than 10 billion pennies out there somewhere right now. But nobody knows exactly where. Because when Canucks turn out their pockets, they find nickels, dimes, and quarters, the odd balled-up lotto ticket, and a fair bit of lint — but darned few pennies.

A recent Gallup poll discovered that the average Canadian carries just four pennies in pocket or purse at any given time. Four pennies times a population of, let's say, 26 million comes out to a little over a hundred million pennies rolling around in circulation. Subtract a hundred million from the 10 billion pennies the Royal Mint says it has punched out . . . and you get some 9 billion, 900 million pennies socked away in pantry drawers, pickle jars, and piggy banks.

Which is why there's a lot of government interest in calling in all those 10 billion pennies and abolishing the coin once and for all.

Personally, I'm opposed to the idea. The penny may not be worth the copper alloy it comes from, but linguistically it's worth its weight in Mastercards. I mean look at the proverbs alone.

"Take care of your pennies and the pounds will take care of themselves."

"Penny saved is a penny earned."

"A penny for your thoughts."

"In for a penny, in for a pound."

"Penny wise and pound foolish."

Oh yes and we've got "Pennies from Heaven" and "Penny Lane" and "Penny Dreadfuls."

So there's some 9 billion, 900 million hoarded pennies out there somewhere. That's, what? Ninety-nine million dollars? And if we managed to winkle all those pennies out from under Aunt Edna's mattress and into circulation again, we could pay for one, maybe one and a half senators?

Nah. We killed the two- and the one-dollar bill. We killed the 50-cent piece. Let the penny alone.

It's just common cents.

Auto Erotica

Now that the Russian bogeyman has been expunged from our nightmares, a lot of pundits are wondering who the next Global Bad Guy is going to be. Gotta have a Global Bad Guy. Otherwise what's the point of having an army and a navy and an air force and several hundred billion dollars' worth of nuclear warheads in our back pocket, right? A Bad Guy is a must. Question is who? Gadhafi's too flaky. Hussein was a flash in the pan. Noriega's been in the slammer for a few years.

Well, not to worry. I believe I've identified the next Terrestrial Supertyrant. And it's not a he. Or a she. It's an it.

The car.

The car is going to be the earthly scapegoat for everything that's wrong with the planet. And it's a near-perfect repository of evil. The car is smelly, kinda clumsy, stays outside, and, aside from the odd honk or rev or tire squeal, doesn't talk back.

Plus it's already got a pretty impressive rap sheet. Quite aside from killing a quarter of a million human beings every year, the automobile scarifies our landscape, destroys neighbourhoods, takes the police away from other more important duties . . . and poisons us. Twenty-five percent of all human-derived carbon dioxide emissions belch out of automobile exhaust pipes.

Then, of course, there's the traffic jam. It used to be an urban phenomenon. Now it's a vehicular fact of life. According to a recent federal report, traffic is only going to get worse. The report says the number of passenger cars has grown more than 70 percent since 1970. There's just one problem: Canada's road system can't be expanded much more. Aside from the expense, we're simply running out of space for extra lanes and overpasses. *Ergo*, more and longer traffic jams in every Canadian's future. Like Germany perhaps. Where thousands of commuters on the Nuremberg–Berlin autobahn got to spend the whole night in a traffic jam recently. They didn't have a lot of choice. The traffic jam was 110 miles long.

Oh yes, the automobile fits the Master Villain profile alright. It's easy to hate the car. Trouble is, we don't. We love the beasts. Their dismal track record is dwarfed by their amazing fertility rate. Car manufacturers around the world are currently turning out new ones at the rate of 100,000 units every day. And they wouldn't be building them if we weren't lining up to buy them.

Newfoundland's ascerbic world philosopher, Gwynne Dyer, gloomily concludes that lots of drivers would rather give up their sex life than their cars.

Maybe we won't have to do either. Perhaps we're poised on the brink of the next automotive technological breakthrough.

Venetian blinds for cars.

Well, we've got to do *something* to while away those impending traffic jams.

The Hockey Stick Forever

Some countries have it easy when it comes to national symbols. The Yanks have the bald eagle. England has the bulldog. Scotland and Ireland have the thistle and shamrock, respectively.

It's not so simple for Canada. The Maple Leaf? It's fine for folks in southern Ontario but it's politically incorrect among the Québécois, and it's a bit of an anomaly on the Prairies, not to mention much of the Maritimes and the great, largely bald rock called Newfoundland.

As for Canadians in the Far North — they seldom see a tree, much less a maple.

Some Canadian communities come up with their own symbols. Sudbury has a giant nickel on its doorstep. The town of Wawa has a fibreglass goose and on the outskirts of Kenora, Ontario, you'll find a humongous muskellunge leaping into the northwestern Ontario skies.

Oh yes, and Toronto has the concrete stalagmite called the CN Tower and Vegreville, Alberta, basks in the shadow of a huge Ukrainian Easter Egg — and these icons are all fine and dandy but . . .

They miss the point, I think. They don't symbolize Canada for ALL Canadians.

There's only one symbol that can truly do that and you'll find it at the town limits of Duncan, British Columbia.

It's a giant hockey stick.

Well, sure. What could be more Canadian? Is it possible that there's a single citizen in this country that wouldn't recognize — *instantly* — a hockey stick?

You don't have to don the skates to be savvy about the lumber. You don't even have to play the game to use one. I haven't hunkered down over a face-off circle in twenty years, but hockey sticks are an important part of my life.

Especially broken ones.

I use them to hold up my tomato plants each summer and to mark the ends of my garden rows. I have also pressed a sawed-off Sherwood Shur-shot into service when a strut in my hammock collapsed a few summers back. Works like a charm.

I've used hockey sticks to scrape snow off my windshield and to "slap-shoot" frozen "calling cards" from the next-door neighbour's German shepherd into aforesaid neighbour's backyard.

Sorry about the one that landed on your barbecue, Fred.

I've always considered myself pretty creative when it comes to finding uses for hockey sticks, but I am a mere babe in the arena compared to Doctor Floydd Mackenzie.

Floydd (yes, there are two ds) is a denizen of Red Deer, Alberta, and the author of a book called *One Hundred and One Ways To Recycle a Hockey Stick*, published by Red Deer College Press. Floydd really has come up with 101 ways to use your basic hockey stick — everything from reaming out eaves troughs to serving as a tiller on a sailboat.

Doctor Mackenzie's book (lavishly illustrated) shows hockey sticks used as fishing rods, leg splints, even emergency kayak paddles (although the kayak does have a tendency to "hook").

Doctor Mackenzie claims that his research has taken him around the globe, chasing down Canada's most famous symbol. He says he's found hockey sticks serving as bootracks in North Dakota, ceiling fan blades in Maine, and tribal masks in the jungles of New Guinea.

The most exotic example of hockey stick recycling in Doctor Mackenzie's book? Well, my favourite among the 101 cited is an easy chair made from two goal sticks and four regular sticks and a welter of meticulously braided hockey tape which the author swears he discovered on a front porch in Stündeskanbe, Sweden.

And I believe him.

Of course, I'm biased.

My wife's relatives all hail from Ürepullenmilaig, Norway.

3

You Were Saying?

What Was the Name Again?

It grieves me to report that Absolutely Nobody passed away last week. No I mean it . . . Absolutely Nobody . . . died last week. He was thirty-seven years old. He lived in Oregon and he answered to the name of Mister Absolutely Nobody. He changed his name and ran for the position of Oregon Lieutenant Governor back in 1991, but he came in third. Which also grieves me. Wouldn't it be wonderful to have a politician you could introduce as the Honourable Absolutely Nobody?

Oh well, at least he lives on in my Goofy Names collection. Right up there with Gertrude Margarete Zelle MacLeod; Mister M. H. Edson Arantes do Nascimento, and Eric Weiss.

Who they? Well, Eric Weiss decided he liked the sound of Houdini better. M. H. Edson Arantes do Nascimento whittled his handle down to a mere four letters and became the famous soccer star Pele. And Gertrude Margarete Zelle MacLeod discovered she got a lot more attention once she started calling herself Mata Hari.

Lots of people change their names for professional reasons. Especially in show business. Tony Curtis was born Bernie Schwartz. Judy Garland was Frances Gumm. Woody Allen's name used to be Allen Stewart Koenigsburg. And can you imagine a two-fisted, six-gun-toting, hard-drinking, hard-riding cowpoke who answers to the name of Marion Morrison? Neither could Hollywood. So they changed it to John Wayne.

Of course, some folks just don't want to change their names. Baseball has some real collectibles. How about Honus Wagner? Yogi Berra? Dusty Rhodes and the late, great Thurman Munson?

They don't all play south of the border, either. Up until a few years ago, the Blue Jays employed a reedy little chap by the name of Rance

Mulliniks to do spot duty. Canadian football gave us Sam Etcheverry and Normie Kwong. Hockey turned up Turk Broda, Eric Nesterenko . . . and my all-time favourite: the modestly talented but magnificently monikered Sheldon Kanageiser.

Some folks change their names for simplification. The case of God comes to mind. He used to be a Californian by the name of Enrique Silberg but Enrique petitioned the court to change his name to God. The court refused, so Enrique compromised. Nowadays he answers to the name Ubiquitous Propinquity God.

For some people their names are already too simple. Like Anthony Mba. Mister Mba is a Nigerian now living in West Hartford, Connecticut. Living and SUING in West Hartford, Connecticut. He's launched a million-dollar harassment suit against a clothing store there in which a sales clerk refused to accept his American Express Gold Card, saying, "Mister MBA? Come on, pal . . . that's not a name, it's a degree!"

All I know is the world has been perceptibly diminished with the passing of Mister Absolutely Nobody, late of Oregon. Gone forever my dream of enticing old Nobody to move up here and run for office, giving us the only palatable candidate on the slate. I don't really see how I can even vote in the next election now. Unless somebody in the Rhino Party runs as Mister None of the Above.

The Importance of the Arts

The first people of Canada attached a lot more importance to names than we do. In the old days, back before we took away their land and rewarded them with a lifetime supply of Bibles, Indians thought long and hard about what they would call their children. They wanted the name to reflect the personality. Thus, it could be months — in some cases, years — before an Indian assumed his given name. Look at the hero in that big Hollywood hit movie of a few years back. He was a middle-aged U.S. cavalryman before the Indians finally got around to naming him "Dances with Wolves."

Well, what's good enough for Kevin Costner is good enough for me. I want a name change.

And I'm not fussy. You can call me "Fumbles with Keyboard" or "Snores in Church" or "He Who Walks About with Fly Unzipped." I don't care what you call me.

As long as it isn't Arthur.

I'm sick of Arthur. I've been lugging it around for more than half a century now, and I never much liked it.

Mind you, I hated it even more when I was a kid. Back then I was "Artie."

It is extremely difficult to establish one's status as a major teenage sex symbol when the family telephone rings, and your sister answers it, then yells, "Artie, some girl wants to talk to you!"

It got worse. Later, I spent a couple of years in England and heard how plummy, upper-class Brits attacked my moniker.

"Awwwwthuh," they called me. Sounded vaguely like a sea lion with indigestion.

Could be worse. At least my parents didn't name me Attila. Or Adolph. Or Oswald, Lee, or Harvey.

Names are fickle. Very few American parents are naming their children George, these days. Just as on this side of the border, newborn males sporting the name of Brian are noticeably scarce.

"Arthur" doesn't carry such a tattered pedigree. Au contraire. There's Artie Shaw and Artur Schopenhauer and Arturo Toscanini.

Not to mention loveable old King Arthur.

And then, of course, there's our great moment of glory in Wardsville, Ontario. True story: Back in the summer of 1983, a government bureaucrat — the assistant deputy minister in the Ontario Ministry of Citizenship and Culture — wrote a letter to all the municipal clerks in the province. Purpose: to ask each clerk to "submit a short brief or letter concerning the Arts in their municipality — how they are regarded, how they are funded, what effect they have on the life or the economy of the municipality . . ."

This is one letter he got back:

Dear Sir:

Reference your letter dated 10 August 1983 requesting information on the Arts in our municipality.

We are pleased to advise that we have four:

Art Harold

Art Morgan

Art Marks

Art Sweet

They are extremely well regarded in the community. They are mostly funded by Old Age Security Pension and Canada Pension, and all contribute to the economy in their day-to-day living.

We are pleased that you are interested in our Arts. However, we have many other names that also deserve recognition, such as William, Charles, Henry, etc., particularly many of the feminine gender, Mary, Helene, Ellen, etc. We would be pleased to forward you a full list if you so wish.

> *Yours truly,*
> *Harold Turton*
> *Clerk,*
> *Village of Wardsville*

There's my answer. I don't have to change my name. I'll just move to Wardsville, where the Arts are really appreciated.

The New Puritanism

The great thing about the future is that it comes just one day at a time.

ABRAHAM LINCOLN

Well, that may have been true in Abe's day, but no more. Nowadays, when I contemplate the future I think of that famous Alex Colville painting — the one that shows an enormous freight train hurtling along the tracks. And running straight towards the oncoming train is a galloping stallion. I think of the train as the future.

I'm the horse.

Or some portion thereof.

The future has never been more overwhelming — or overlapping. Consider: there are people alive right now who were born before a single airplane or television signal sullied the heavens.

Let's ponder something much smaller than that. Let's ponder the letters "P" and "C."

When I was born, "PC" stood for a flatfoot, a cop, a patrolman.

As in "Police Constable O'Casey apprehended the miscreant and took him down to the station."

A little later in my life, "PC" took on party affiliation: Progressive Conservative. John Diefenbaker was a PC. So was Robert Stanfield and Flora MacDonald and Kim . . . Kim . . .

Oh, you know who I mean.

Then, just a few years ago, "PC" underwent another metamorphosis. Suddenly, "PC" no longer described that herd of brontosaurs grazing mindlessly on the far right edge of the Canadian political savannah — now it was the designation for a mysterious slab of molded plastic that unfolded to reveal a screen and a keyboard.

Enter "PC" — the Personal Computer.

And while I was still struggling to find the ON switch of my laptop, damned if the letters didn't hopscotch into the void only to reappear in yet another incarnation.

Nowadays, "PC" stands for "Politically Correct."

It's the new Puritanism and it's raging like a forest fire through the groves of Academe. Squads of self-appointed PC Thought Police scour the dorms and the classrooms for any sign of deviation from the Gospel According to Political Correctness.

Thus, a professor at Harvard is taken to task for dwelling on Shakespeare, Milton, and Blake (Dead White Males are not Politically Correct).

Thus, a private Catholic hospital in Oak Park, Illinois, is not allowed to erect a cross on its own smokestack because, according to the town council, "some local residents would be offended."

It gets sillier than that. A merchandise catalogue featuring a drawing of Porky Pig urging customers, "D-d-d-don't delay: D-d-do your holiday shopping today," attracted the wrath of a Stutterers' Rights group. The merchandiser promised to drop Porky in the next edition.

Remember the reissue of the Disney classic movie *Fantasia*? Well, listen to the rap sheet that cartoon's racked up: Dieters United objected to the depiction of tutu-clad hippos, saying it ridiculed fat people; radical conservationists protested the conspicuous waste of water in the "Sorcerer's Apprentice" section; an anti-drug lobbyist railed that the dancing mushrooms in the *Nutcracker Suite* portion were clearly hallucinogenic.

Oh yes, and one child was frightened by the graphics that accompanied "Night on Bald Mountain."

Personally, I'm hoping that "PC" will reinvent itself again before the PC Nazis gain much more ground. Some "PC" thing that will evolve smoothly and naturally out of the Political Correctness movement as we know it.

May I suggest Pure Crap?

Words — Warts and All

Write me off as a singular bore if you want, but I am sublimely uninterested in "gender-neutral" language.

It's all the rage, you know. Shepherds and shepherdesses are *verboten*. The term is "herdperson." You're not even supposed to say "chairwoman" or "chairman" anymore. The officially laundered and approved phrase is "chairperson" — or simply "the chair."

Well, sorry, Ms. Grundy, but "the chair" is what I park "the bum" in. And as for gender fuzzification, I think it's just another ploy for lawyers and politicians and other paper-spewing windbags who pay their mortgages by muddying up the water the rest of us have to swim through.

The English language is a marvellous creation — a bottomless quiver full of razor-sharp adjectival arrows honed and edged for every imaginable target. We have so many glorious words — masculine and feminine. Why would anyone want to neutralize them?

The scary thing about these self-appointed language gelders is that they just might win. If we don't use words we lose them. If you don't believe me, go ask your kids what a "throttle," a "treadle," or "Wellingtons" are. Sure, you know — but I bet they don't.

There was a time when we cared a great deal more about words. Back in the fifteenth century, a language maven by the name of Dame Juliana Berners published *The Book of St. Albans*. It was a small book — a manual, really — consisting of 164 specific terms for groups of things. We can thank Dame Juliana for a "pride" of lions and a "litter" of puppies; for a "swarm" of bees and a "flock" of sheep.

This book first differentiated between geese on the ground ("gaggle") and geese in the air ("skein").

For the past five hundred years, thanks to *The Book of St. Albans*, English speakers have referred to "slates" of candidates and "herds" of elephants.

We even kept the mistakes Dame Juliana made. She insisted that the correct term for a group of fish was "school." Actually, it was misspelling of "shoal," but as nobody spelled very well in the fifteenth century, Dame Juliana's word was as good as anybody's and better than most.

Some of her descriptions are pure poetry. How better to describe a mass of locusts than a "plague"?

And birds — how about:

> *A bouquet of pheasants?*
> *A murder of crows?*
> *A parliament of owls?*
> *A brood of hens?*
> *An exaltation of larks?*

Dame Juliana didn't deal exclusively in animal codification. She also gave us:

> *A sentence of judges*
> *An impatience of wives*
> *A boast of soldiers*
> *An impertinence of peddlers*
> *A drift of fishermen*
> *An eloquence of lawyers*

Too bad Dame Juliana's not around today. We've got some brand new groups that just cry out for codification. How about:

> *A sleaze of politicians?*
> *A rant of evangelists?*
> *An ooze of salesmen?*

And, of course, *an eternity of columnists* — especially ones with (a swarm of) bees in their bonnets about words.

Looking For a Fall Guy? You're It, Buddy

The world has benefitted greatly from the Jews. They gave us the Torah and Doctor Seuss. They also gave us Albert Einstein and Lenny Bruce; Yehudi Menuhin and Bob Dylan; bagels and lox.

But I think the greatest gift the Jews bestowed upon us was the concept of the scapegoat.

You can read about it in the Bible. It tells us that on the Day of Atonement, Aaron selected two goats. One was slaughtered ritually as a sacrifice to the Lord. Then Aaron turned to the other goat and said something like: "You! Look at you! You call yourself a goat? You're a joke! A disgrace to goatdom! Not only that but I hereby saddle you with all the sins and transgressions my people have committed in the past year. My people are now pure and innocent. You, on the other hand, are a mess. Now get outta here already!"

And the goat was banished. Driven into the wilderness.

Which personally I think is a helluva lot preferable to having your throat slit on an altar, but that's not the point. The point is: This ritual gave the world the principle of the "scapegoat" — picking some poor schnook out of the crowd and blaming him, her, or it for everything that's bad.

Mankind has been using scapegoats ever since. The English treated the Highland Scots and the Irish as scapegoats. The Nazis did the same to the Gypsies and the Jews.

On a less bloodthirsty scale we all use scapegoats. The Newfie joke, the Mulroney dartboard, the Toronto Maple Leafs — all variations on the scapegoat theme.

Trouble is, good scapegoats are getting hard to find. The Toronto Maple Leafs are beginning to play respectable hockey. Brian Mulroney is mostly living in Palm Springs and staying out of our lives. And Newfie jokes just ain't funny.

It is no longer politically correct to wax lighthearted about ethnics, gays, or women. Hell, you can get in trouble telling jokes about folks who are short or bal . . . oops — I mean follically challenged.

As a matter of fact, there's a politician in Albany, New York, who tried to get a law passed "banning weight bigotry." If Assemblyman Daniel Feldman had his way, any employer who refused to hire someone as . . . oh, say, a ballerina or a fashion model or a trapeze artist, just because said person is built like, and weighs as much as, a Dodge Minivan — well, that employer would be subject to prosecution.

As I said, it's getting tough to find a decent scapegoat these days.

But I think I've managed to turn one up. A scapegoat, I mean. I found it in the pages of *Harpers Magazine*.

It was an ad for a book by June Stephenson. The ad copy says, "Why do so many boys grow up to be criminals? Whether it's murder, rape or the S&L scandal, crime costs $300 billion a year. Prison inmates are 94 percent male. Why is crime essentially a male pursuit? Read MEN ARE NOT COST EFFECTIVE: Male Crime in America."

There you have it, kiddies. The perfect patsy. No question of race or religion, or custom or belief or short or tall or fat or skinny. Just . . . man, the fall guy. Half the human race ready, waiting, and practically crying out to be pronounced Guilty As Charged.

Hey, don't laugh. It's already happening. The Lingo Police are out there as I write, scouring the English tongue to eradicate every filthy foxhole of male-tainted language. We've got personhole covers in the streets now. We've got herdpersons and fisherpersons and if you think I exaggerate, go look it up.

In your Herstory book.

Man. The ultimate scapegoat.

I'd whine some more but I've gotta go. I promised I'd meet my buddies out in the wilderness for a couple of beers.

Could You Spell That, Please?

There's a famous old Broadway song by George and Ira Gershwin that contains the plaintive lament:

> *Eether, eyether,*
> *Neether, nyether,*
> *Let's call the whole thing off.*

The Gershwin boys had tapped into something that makes the English language one of the most baffling, infuriating — and delightful — adventures a human tongue can undertake.

Pronunciation. When it comes to English you might as well throw the rule book out the window. Although if it goes through and lands on a rough bough, try not to cough.

The last sentence used five words that end in "ough." Each one of them is pronounced differently.

And it's not just words ending in "ough." I grew up just down the street from a kid named Bruce Kahoon.

I thought.

I was astounded one day when I saw his last name written out properly. It was spelled Colquohoun.

I have two friends with the surname MacKay, but one pronounces it Mac-Hi and the other says Mac-Hay.

Then, of course, there's MacLeod (pronounced Mac-lowd) and McKeown (pronounced Mick-Yew-en) and McLaughlin and McCullough and McEachern and . . .

Well, you get the idea.

Some of the odd pronunciations are totally baffling. Others have perfectly good explanations. The story behind the Scottish name of

Home, for instance. During the sixteenth-century Battle of Flodden Field, Lord Home was one of the Scottish nobles who tried to rally his troops to drive back the Sassenachs. Lord Home began waving a banner and shouting his name, "Home! Home! Home!"

His soldiers heard the shouts, thought it sounded like a good idea, turned on their heels, and headed for home.

The story goes that the next day Lord Home decreed that the family name would henceforth be pronounced "Hyoom."

Not that the Scots have any corner on the wonky pronunciation sweepstakes. In Britain you can find the rather magnificent family moniker Cholmondeley.

It's pronounced Chumley.

There is also Magdalen College in Oxford.

Pronounced Mawdlin.

And Worcester is Wooster and Leicester is Lester and Ulgham is Uff-im and how do you think you pronounce a place on the south coast of England named Mousehole?

Should be fairly straightforward, should it not? We have mouseholes in Canada, don't we?

Except the British one is pronounced Mow-zul.

Strange pronunciations can trip up even the pros. There's a story told in the halls of the Canadian Broadcasting Corporation concerning how the late, great Lorne Green early in his career as an announcer once bungled a weather forecast on CBC radio.

The script gave the highs and lows for an Ontario town named Kapuskasing.

When Lorne read it, it came out Ka PUS kasing.

Oh well, no surprise in a country that has a city spelled Toronto but pronounced Trawnna and a province that looks like it should be pronounced Kew beck but is properly pronounced Kay Bek.

Could be worse. We could have Spanish pronunciations to contend with, the way they do south of the border.

There's a story about a loud New York tourist stopping at a restaurant on the outskirts of Mexia, Texas, buttonholing a waitress and braying, "Now lissen, honey. I want you to say very slowly and very clearly the name of this place we're in okay?" The waitress says, "Sure," takes a deep breath, looks right in the tourist's eyes, and yells very carefully, "Daaaaaaairy Queeeeeeeeen."

Robert Burns:
A Man for a' That

Okay folks, come on now . . .

Stop hassling blacks. Quit bugging the Jews. Get off the backs of Indians and Albanians and South Africans and Germans. You want a race to pick on? Let me offer my own motley tribe — the Scots.

Why not? What have the Scots ever given us? They have given us . . . the kilt — for which no man in his right mind in a cold draft could say a kind word.

They have given us . . . the bagpipes, which, when played expertly by a master, still sound like a sack full of alley cats going through drug withdrawal.

The Scots have given us the exquisitely masochistic game of golf, in which, as Winston Churchill once said, one endeavours to control a ball with implements ill-adapted for the purpose.

The Scots have also given us porridge, Presbyterianism, Calvinism, and, thanks to Alexander G. Bell, that greatest of twentieth-century pains in the ear — the telephone. Those are a few of the things that Scots have done for us. What else — whiskey? Nonsense. God invented whiskey. Mankind's original safety belt — to restrain the Scots from taking over the world.

Oh, it's a scathing indictment we could lay at the feet of Scotland were it not for one wee sleekit mitigating factor. One other present from the Scots. They did give us Rabbie Burns.

Robert Burns. Born 1759, died 1796. As career trajectories go, not a long one — a mere thirty-seven years. Not a particularly pretty one, either — he died of heart disease brought on in part by a lifetime of too much hard work fuelled by bad food.

The most remarkable thing about Burns is that he was so untypically

Scottish. The Scots of the late eighteenth century were (some would argue, still are) dour and sober and pious and gloomy. Burns was robust and rollicky, passionate and rebellious. He blasphemed the church by writing a scathing poem to a local hypocritical clergyman, a poem called "Holy Willie's Prayer." He scandalized the neighbours with bawdy songs and unsanctified liaisons with Elizabeth. And Jean. And Agnes. And Jenny. And Meg. And Highland Mary.

Scotland had not seen his like before — and certainly not since. A dark, muscular ploughman turned poet. But such a poet. Listen to the reviews. "What an antithetical mind! — tenderness, roughness — delicacy, coarseness — sentiment, sensuality — soaring and grovelling — dirt and deity — all mixed up in that one compound of inspired clay!" That, from Lord Byron.

"Burns had a real heart of flesh and blood beating in his bosom — you can almost hear it throb. Someone said, that if you had shaken hands with him, his hand would have burnt yours." That, from William Hazlitt.

"Burns of all poets is the most a man." That, from Dante Rossetti.

Pity his countrymen didn't think so — but then Burns was not a civilized man. He drank too much and talked too loud and spent his money foolishly and his affections recklessly . . . but he wrote some of the loveliest love poems that have ever been penned. And wouldn't you die to have spent an afternoon with him on the banks of the Afton?

Read the words to "A Red, Red Rose" or "Sweet Afton" or "A Man's a Man for a' That" — and it's hard to believe that the man who wrote them would be more than two and a half centuries old if he was alive, but it's true.

Next New Year's Eve you might consider taking a wee dram of kindness in memory of the man who gave us "Auld Lang Syne."

Sam Johnson: Wordsmith

I'm looking at a portrait of Samuel Johnson, 1709–84, author of that monumental first dictionary of the English language.

I don't know what a lexicographer is supposed to look like, but I'm pretty sure Samuel Johnson wasn't it. He was a big man — portly and burly. His face was pitted and pockmarked from scrofula. He also suffered from dropsy, asthma, and gout, and he was partially blind and half deaf. Oh, yes, and a terminal glutton to boot. He liked a drink — alcoholic and otherwise. Was known to knock back up to twenty-five cups of tea at a sitting. One observer tells of Sam Johnson tucking into his roast beef with such intensity that the veins on his forehead bulged and sweat beaded on his brow. Not surprisingly, Doctor Johnson often complained of stomach pains, flatulence, catarrh, and high blood pressure, too. He dressed like a vagabond and walked like a *coureur de bois* with a curious, rolling lurch.

With all his afflictions, though, Samuel Johnson managed to make it to the age of seventy-five. Which is a miracle. A miracle that nobody murdered him before that.

Because Sam Johnson had a tongue on him. And he used it the way Cecil Fielder uses a baseball bat. There were a lot of people Sam didn't like and he wasn't shy about announcing it. He despised, for instance, the Scots. "Much may be made of a Scotchman — if he is caught young."

He disparaged citizens of the U.S.: "I am willing to love all mankind, except an American."

He made mock of anglers: "A fishing rod is a stick with a hook at one end and a fool at the other."

And he was the ultimate male chauvinist porker when it came to women. Sam Johnson it was who poo-pooed a tale about a marvellous woman preacher with the observation, "Sir, a woman's preaching is like a dog walking on his hind legs. It is not done well, but you are surprised to find it done at all."

Well, it was the 1700s after all. I mean, the original chauvinist, Nicholas Chauvin, hadn't even been born yet.

Doctor Johnson talked in that Major Hoople harumph-harumph style — loud, somewhat pompous, and stagey. "Depend upon it, sir, when a man knows he is to be hanged in a fortnight, it concentrates the mind wonderfully."

Poor old Johnson. Spent eleven years of his life putting together that first dictionary. Today, it looks mighty thin, up there beside the Oxfords and the Funk and Wagnalls and the Gages. Not much more than a curiosity, really. As are most of Johnson's serious works. The poems, the tragedies, and essays. His style (orotund) and his mood (gloomy) mean that most modern readers take only very selected and circumspect dips into the vast body of Johnsonian writings.

Which was a dangerous thing to do when the Great Man himself was around. Shortly after his dictionary was published, two very proper ladies approached Johnson and complimented him — especially on the fact that his book omitted all vulgar, lewd, and licentious words.

"What, my dears?" bellowed Doctor Johnson. "Then you've been looking for them!"

How Not To Get Hired

One of the luxuries of being middle-aged or older is that you can look back on all the jobs you've held.

And glory in the knowledge that you don't have to do them any more.

Back in the Bad Old Days there were jobs galore. The pay was usually lousy, the working conditions ran the gamut from dreary to downright dangerous, and the boss as often as not was a jerk.

But that was okay. You took the job for as long as you needed it, then one fine day you told your esteemed employer to pound Sifto, and off you went to find another job.

I counted them up once and discovered I had twenty-seven different kinds of jobs before I finally manacled myself to a word processor for life. I tried everything from door-to-door encyclopedia flogging to swabbing the deck of a Liberian oil tanker.

Being a job gypsy doesn't make you rich, but it does give you plenty to talk about.

The other day I was in a bar, jawing with another Jackrabbit of All Trades. We wound up comparing our work wounds — Softest Jobs. Best Paying Jobs. Jobs We'd Like To Have Again.

And All-Time Worst Jobs.

"Roofing," I told him. "Tar and gravel. Started at five in the morning and worked until at least three guys fainted from the heat or the fumes. Put a thermometer on the roof one day and the mercury shot right off the scale in less than a minute. Still got scars on my arms from the hot pitch. Get thirsty just thinking about that job," I said. "How about you?"

He was a battered-looking guy with big callous-hardened mitts and twitchy eyes that looked like they were sitting on a lot of secrets. I figured he'd come back with a story about digging for emeralds in the jungles of Brazil or rearranging kneecaps in the jungles of New Jersey.

His big fist trembled as he reached for the draft glass and his voice dropped to a husky mutter.

"Personnel recruiter," he croaked. "Toughest job I ever had."

Turned out he'd spent two and a half years screening recruits for a large Toronto corporation. "Before that I'd worked the oil fields in Alberta, tugboats in the Georgia Strait, and a spell of hardrock mining in Manitouwadge — but the only job that ever gave me an ulcer was a desk job on Bay Street."

I thought he was pulling my leg, but maybe not. I'm beginning to think that interviewing prospective employees may be one of the toughest gigs a guy can draw.

I have in front of me a list compiled from a survey conducted by the International Association of Corporate and Professional Recruiters. The Association asked its six hundred members to list some of the more "unusual questions" they'd been asked by people looking for a job.

Here's a few of the choice ones:

"Why am I here?"

"Why aren't you in a more interesting business?"

"What are the zodiac signs of all the board members and their wives?"

"What is it that you people do at this company?"

"Would it be a problem if I'm angry most of the time?"

"Does the company have a policy regarding whether employees can carry guns?"

"Will the company pay for moving my two-ton rock garden from California to Maryland?"

And my favourite: "I know this is off the subject, but will you marry me?"

Puts a whole new perspective on that beady-eyed guy sitting on the other side of the personnel desk, doesn't it?

Yessir . . . I've been a roofer, a sailor, a cattle prodder, and a bartender, but I've never been a personnel recruiter and I'm glad of it.

I don't think I'm tough enough.

"I'm Sorry, Smith —
You've Been
Transitioned"

Ever been fired? I have, once or twice. It's a bracing experience. Rather like being shot by a large invisible Air Cannon. YOU'RE FIRED. (THUMP.) Ooof! The shock is visceral. If you're supremely cool, you might manage to say something clever, or cutting or defiant, but most of us are more lamb than lion. Hard of hearing mutton at that — "What? What did you say? Did you say 'fired?'" After that it's just a case of getting out of the room. Hoping that your knees work, your lunch stays down, and your pants stay dry.

A lot of Canadians getting fired these days — although it's seldom called that anymore. Now wage earners are plucked from payrolls by a whole host of weasel-worded philosophies like "streamlining," "down-sizing," and "work force outplacement."

It's a pity. To be told you're fired may be painful, but at least it's honest. Far better than being informed that you are being destaffed, redeployed, separated involuntarily, transitioned, or work force adjusted. I am not making those up. They come from a list of terms actually used by corporations when firing employees, published in a newsletter called *Executive Recruiter News*. I am also not making up the news release from Digital Equipment Corporation, a company that recently lopped nearly 3,500 employees off the payroll. Wholesale firings? Not at all. "Involuntary methodologies" was the term the company press release used.

It must be doubly insulting to be simultaneously fired and bullshat upon. I think most people would prefer the news straight. "Getting fired" has fine, old Anglo-Saxon roots. It refers to the ancient custom of driving unwelcome visitors away with flaming brands. "Getting sacked" has even more bloodthirsty origins. That goes back to the

1500s when a persona non grata was routinely trussed up in a sack and pitched into the sea.

Still, losing a regular paycheque is pretty blunt. Feels a lot closer to getting fired or sacked than it does to getting excessed, executively decruited, or subjected to a reshaping skill-mix adjustment.

If it has to happen, then far better to be out-front fired, canned, axed, dumped, or given the chop. As an old boss once told me, if you've got to suck a lemon, suck it fast.

Excuse Me

There is hardly a man so strict as not to vary when he is to make an excuse.

LORD HALIFAX

Very sorry can't come to dinner. Lie follows by post.

TELEGRAM FROM LORD BERESFORD TO KING EDWARD

Ah, the humble excuse. Could modern civilization function without the veritable vermicelli of little white lies we all tell to get out of things we don't want to do each and every day? Probably not. It's early morning as I type this, but already I've fended off a flock of Jehovah's Witnesses by telling them I'm a practising Buddhist; I've deflected a telephone sales pitch for magazine subscriptions by claiming I'm stone blind; and I've promised my boon companion and faithful cohort that, you bet, for sure I'll get those storm windows off this afternoon, first thing.

Just as soon as this twinge in my back eases off.

Lies, all lies. Well, not lies, exactly. Excuses. Little dabs of social lubricant that help to smooth the meshing gears of everyday life.

An awful lot of impressive human creativity goes into making excuses — sometimes we expend more mental sweat trying to avoid a job than we would if we just went ahead and did the damned thing — but that's human nature, too. And sometimes the excuses themselves become somewhat twisted works of Art.

Consider, for example, the excuse of glamour girl Zsa Zsa Gabor, explaining why she slugged a Beverly Hills cop when he ticketed her for driving with expired plates on her Rolls Royce:

"I am from Hungary. We are descendants of Genghis Khan and Attila the Hun. We are Hungarian Freedom Fighters."

Or how about Chrysler shill Lee Iacocca, making excuses for not cleaning up automobile emissions:

"We've got to ask ourselves: how much clean air do we need?"

Then there's Jessica Hahn, Jimmy Bakker's ex-playtoy, excusing herself for doing a ten-page, full-colour nude layout in Playboy:

"It brought me closer to God."

Not as famous, but just as inventive, is the spokesman for the U.S. defence contractor, Pratt and Whitney, desperately trying to excuse the fact that his company charged the Pentagon $999 for pliers. That is, $999 for *each pair.*

Explained the spokesman: "Well, they're multi-purpose pliers."

Anyone who starts off most of his sentences with a long, drawn-out "Welllllll," is bound to be a good excuse-maker. Former U.S. president Ronald Reagan proves the point. His excuse to Chief of Staff Jim Baker for not reading his briefing notes for an important economic summit meeting: "Wellll, Jim, *The Sound of Music* was on last night."

And then there's Bill Clinton's classic — an excuse that will go down in the annals of Born Again Pot Smokers Everywhere:

"I didn't like it and I didn't inhale it."

My all-time favourite excuse? I give the nod to Lighton Ndefwayl. Mister Ndefwayl isn't a household name in Canada, but he is in Zambia, where he's known as the best tennis player that country ever produced.

Until 1993, that is. In '93, Mister Ndefwayl was defeated by another Zambian tennis player — one Musumba Bwayla.

Mind you, Mister Ndefwayl had an excuse for his loss. "Musumba Bwayla is a stupid man," said Ndefwayl, "— and a hopeless player. He has a big nose and is cross-eyed. Girls hate him. He beat me because my jockstrap was too tight and because when he serves, he farts, and that made me lose my concentration for which I am famous throughout Zambia."

Well, perhaps so, Mister Ndefwayl, but you're still the number two tennis player in Zambia.

According to the last report.

English: A World-Class Language

*P*arlez vous anglais? Habla ingles? Sprechen sie Englische? A lot of people do. It's a feisty and fecund little language we've attached ourselves to, we Anglophones. According to the *Cambridge Encyclopedia of Language,* close to two billion human beings use or understand the English language. It's the official or semi-official tongue in more than sixty modern nations . . . and you can easily get by speaking English in another twenty.

The numbers seem to be going up, rather than down. In Russia you can go into many businesses nowadays and ask to see the "mene-dzher." Chances are you'll find him sitting in front of his "kom pyuturr."

And in Paris, L'Académie française has finally thrown in the white handkerchief. L'Académie is an august gathering of French intellectuals empowered to actually decree which new words are or are not worthy of inclusion in the French language. L'Académie française, which for years had been defending the French barricades against the onslaught of the barbarian Anglais, has officially — *Faites attention, s'il vous plaît* — adopted — le drugstore, le bulldozer, le cowboy, and le dead heat.

The strength of our language is that it comes in such bewildering varieties. There's not just British English and American English. There's Hindu English, South African English, Rasta English, Maori English . . . why there's even Canadian English.

When the Blue Jays first made it to the World Series a few years back, the American newsmagazine *Newsweek* felt compelled to offer a lexicon of Canadian English, just in case some American ball fans should lose their scouts or outriders and find themselves *in terra incognita* around the Toronto Skydome. Thus, said *Newsweek*, it was important in Canada to demand a two-four when buying a case of beer, to show compassion for anyone "collecting pogey," and under no circumstances to inflame the natives by giving them the Trudeau salute.

Ah, yes . . . English is everywhere. Even in Japan, one of the most seamless and impenetrable cultures on the planet.

In the Tokyo business district, executives in "manejimento" now take breaks from riding herd on the "mane-sapurai" (money supply) to watch a game of "besoboru."

On a sadder note, some Japanese are learning a whole new litany of English words, thanks to a tragedy in Louisiana a few Halloweens ago. A Japanese exchange student on his way to a party approached the wrong house and ran into an America-Firster with a handgun. "Freeze!" snarled the homeowner. "Freeze?" thought the Japanese exchange student? "I don't underst —" *BAM.*

In response, a Japanese newspaper printed a list of "tourist phrases" visitors to the U.S. may need to understand in order to survive. The handy phrases include: "Stick 'em up"; "Spread 'em"; "Don't move a muscle"; "Hands in the air"; and "Move and die."

Ah, the Americans. Mel Brooks once said to Barbara Frum: "Please tender my regards to all the citizens of Canada. They do not say, 'house' or 'mouse' — they say, 'hoose' and 'moose'. I love it. And I think they are taller than Americans, they are kinder, and they are more gentle."

Well, I don't know about all that. But I do know that if you're a stranger in this strange land and a Canadian says, "Freeze," he's only talking about the weather. You don't have to fear for your life. Not right away, anyway.

Heard These Words Yet?

"I was grooving to this Rap CD on my Walkman last night down by the video store when suddenly this Yuppie blindsides me and rips a big hole in my Gore-Tex — bummer."

What — aside from an undisguised whiff of air-headedness on the part of the speaker — is wrong with the preceding sentence?

Answer: not a thing. Except if you'd said it to John George Diefenbaker when he was alive, he'd probably have sicced the Mounties on you as a suspected extraterrestrial. When Dief the Chief died, the world had not yet seen Rap, CDs, Walkmans, or video stores. Yuppies still hadn't been invented and neither had Gore-Tex.

And Diefenbaker died in 1979. Less than a generation ago.

We've got a lot of English additions that would make old John George shake his wattles in confusion. He wouldn't know what to make of AIDS or insider trading. Or sunblock or Poop-and-Scoop laws either.

Nuclear winter . . . Infotainment . . . Pay per view . . . Mid-life crisis . . . might as well be speaking Martian to anyone who checked out in the seventies.

That's the wonderful thing about the English language: It's always changing, never still. It is forever taking on new words and phrases, custom-fitting them for our ears.

But language is a two-way street. A lot of old words and phrases get discarded to make room for the new. Our grandfathers grew up in a world of spats and spittoons, speakeasies and spliced mainbraces.

Today, there's not one kid in a thousand who could explain any of those terms.

Remember the cliché "lock, stock, and barrel," meaning everything connected with some object or process? Don't try it out on anyone under thirty. They'll have no idea what you're talking about. Try "the whole nine yards" instead — as in "Yeah, I bought the deluxe model . . . air conditioning, power windows, tinted glass . . . the whole nine yards."

English is so doggone powerful it invades other languages at will. The French speak of leaving "le camping car" at "un parking" at the airport to clamber aboard "le jumbo jet." Germans, who call their employer "der Boss," often spend their leisure hours dressed in running shorts and sneakers, engaged in "das Joggen." Italians seem more attracted to "il bodybuilding."

A lot of languages borrow from English. Sometimes I wish we'd return the favour. Foreign tongues have a lot of words and expressions our language just can't match.

Such as? Well, such as the French expression *esprit d'escalier*, which translates as "the spirit of the staircase." It refers to the clever retort you could have made to the smartass at the party — except you didn't think of it until you were on your way home — virtually going "up the staircase."

The Germans have an expression that we could dearly use. You know those annoyingly narrow-minded technocrats who never foresee the consequences of their work? The agriculturalists who pushed DDT because it increased crop yield? The government economic flacks who advocate nuclear power because it's "efficient"? The Germans have a word for them. They call them *Fachidiots*.

Close enough to English to be richly satisfying in two languages.

Let me conclude by introducing you to another linguistic newborn. Remember former U.S. president George Bush's disastrous trip to Japan a few years back during which he upchucked on the Japanese prime minister? It's given the Japanese a new word: *Bushusuru*. They use it to describe the curious custom of Japanese businessmen power drinkers. These are guys who get stinking drunk as fast as they can. Then they stagger down the nearest alley . . .

And *Bushusuru* all over the place.

Woops! The Woopies Have Landed

The baby boom is twice as big as the generation that pre-ceded it. It's like a deer going through a boa constrictor. You don't notice anything the snake ate before or after. They're the biggest game in town and they will be until they die.

WASHINGTON SOCIOLOGIST

And we're a long way from dying, we baby boomers. As a matter of fact we're just beginning to hit the half-century mark. Experts estimate that within the next three decades, the number of North Americans over the age of fifty will skyrocket by 80 percent. Every third person you meet will be fifty or older.

It's more than a North American phenomenon. The Japanese are "silvering" even faster. So are Western Europeans.

But we're not just accumulating wrinkles and cellulite saddle bags, we aging baby boomers. We also, according to the experts, pack a fair amount of scratch. In fact, surveys show that the over-fifties already have as much spending loot as all other age groups put together.

Needless to say, the advertisers have sniffed out and homed in on this phenomenon like a school of piranha on a bleeding pig.

The marketers have studied us, subdivided us into "age groups" . . . they've even come up with a brand new name for us.

It's kind of silly to call something that's half a century old a "baby" anything. So we're not baby boomers anymore. Or Yuppies. Or teeny boppers.

We're Woopies.

It stands for Well-Off Older People — and if you are one, hang on to your hairpiece because you are about to be media blitzed like you've never been blitzed before.

You may have noticed some of the advertising changes already. There's a clothing company out there offering "roomier" jeans — pants that don't look like they've been put on with a spray gun. That's because the jean manufacturers realize that our bodies aren't what they once were. We don't want flaunting clothes — we want camouflage. Naturally, the jeans are selling like hotcakes.

Not that all the new marketing ideas are successful. A few are downright duds. Some American telephone companies introduced "silver pages" — listings for goods and services specifically aimed at the older section of the populace. Woopies wanted nothing to do with them.

A couple of years ago, Johnson & Johnson introduced a new shampoo for "older hair." It grew cobwebs on the shelves. Woopies don't want their oldness rubbed in their face. So Johnson & Johnson scrapped the ads and wrote some new ones that promised the shampoo would make hair "alluring at any age." Sales took off.

Seems like Woopies are very sensitive about language. They're happy to consider living in an "adults only" environment — but don't want to be caught dead in a "retirement community."

Well, I'm sensitive about language, too — particularly when it's employed by pussyfooting snake oil salesmen trying to separate me from my pathetic little hoard of loonies.

So, as I totter into Woopiedom, a word of advice to all those honey-tongued hucksters out there in media land:

Don't call me a Senior Citizen. Don't call me a Golden Ager or an Oldster.

And for God's sake don't you dare call me Chronologically Endowed.

As a matter of fact, don't call me at all.

I plan to be extremely busy for the rest of my days.

Making whoopie.

What's in a Name?

The most popular I'm told, is David for boys, Linda for girls. The least popular according to a U.S. survey . . . well, don't call your kids Faber or Temperance if you want them to have a career in public life. Schuyler, Malig, and Lola May are also near universal turnoffs, moniker-wise.

I'm talking about people's names. I've been pondering this for a few years now. Ever since I heard the news that an up-and-coming Hollywood actor had up and died. It wasn't so much that he died; it was the fact that his name was River Phoenix. Not only that, he had a brother named Leaf. Or is it a sister? Who's to say?

Odd what parents will saddle their kids with. I got my middle name from one of my dad's army buddies. My sister carries our grandmother's name. Edna St. Vincent Millay got her middle name from a New York hospital that saved her mother's brother's life.

Longest name that actually appears on a birth certificate? That would belong to Rhoshandia Tellynishiaun Neveshenk Koya Ann Fsquatsiuty Williams, beloved daughter of Mister and Missus Jim Williams of Beaumont, Texas. At least that was the longest up until October of 1984. That's when papa Jim filed an amendment expanding his daughter's first name to a modest nine-hundred-odd extra letters. We don't have space.

Nor do we have time to go through the first names of Don Alfonso de Borbòn y Borbòn, the great-great grandson of Spanish King Carlos the Third. Don Alfonso had 94 official first names — which pales beside Laurence Watkins of Auckland, New Zealand. Mister Watkins answers . . . eventually . . . to 2,310 first names.

Then there are patriotic names. Back in the early days of the Russian revolution (I mean the original Russian revolution), Melor was a very popular name to lay on one's little babushka. M.E.L.O.R. — an anagram for Marx Engels Lenin October Revolution.

Hey, it scans better than the strange virus of mechanically patriotic name tagging that swept Cuba after Fidel took over — where you can still find grown-up children of the revolution who answer to names like Propela and Biela — meaning propellor and connecting rod.

As for the nonrevolutionized world, I don't know whether it signifies the decline of royalty or not, but monarchical names these days lack the flair they once had. Queen Elizabeth and Princess Anne — that's pretty tame stuff compared to William the Conqueror, Ivan the Terrible, John the Perfect Prince.

Not that royalty was automatically revered. History also reveals Charles the Bald, Ferdinand the Fickle, Henry the Impotent, and Rudolph the Sluggard.

Plus my favourite . . . John the Posthumous.

Talk about laidback.

Most common name in all the world? Well, what do you figure? David, maybe? Linda? John, possibly?

Nope. It's Chang. About 10 percent of the Chinese population answer to that name. That works out to upwards of 104 million individual Changs. The most common English surname is Smith but it doesn't even come close to Chang — there's less than 3 million Smiths in all of North America.

Lot of folks think that you've got it made if you have a famous name, but I can tell you it just isn't so. I know that Conrad has often spoken despairingly of the burden he shoulders with his surname. People constantly badgering him, asking him does he know me? Could he possibly get my autograph?

It's not easy sharing a famous name. Charles Edison found that out. He was the politician son of the famous inventor Thomas Edison . . . and Charles went to great lengths to dissociate himself from his world-renowned father. "I would not have anyone believe I am trading on the name Edison," he would explain in his campaign speeches. "I would rather have you know me merely as one of my father's earlier experiments."

Factoids — Who Needs 'Em?

Here's a new word for you. Actually, it's not brand new, but it is young. Not much more than a teenager. Spawned, as near as anyone can figure, in a festering slime bog within spitting distance of Washington's Capitol Hill, back in the mid-seventies.

The word is *factoid*. It's so new that a lot of dictionaries don't yet list it. But if you find one that does, it'll say something like:

> **fac-toid** (fak'toid) *n. something fictitious or unsubstantiated that is presented as fact and accepted because of constant repetition.*

Yup, that's the factoid alright. You hear all kinds of factoids in sports — you know the ones I mean.

You're watching a duller-than-average Blue Jays game on TV. No score, bottom of the third, Joe Carter's at the plate. Suddenly the commentator murmurs, "Y'know, Don, it's interesting to realize that over his career, Carter's got himself on base 87.5 percent of the time, when facing a left-handed pitcher chewing tobacco in the bottom of the third inning . . ."

Scaremongers love to throw factoids around. "Canadians," someone will intone ominously, "drink enough beer each year to fill 312 Olympic swimming pools."

Or, "If all the cigarettes smoked from 1979 to 1992 by North American females between the ages of thirteen and sixty-three were laid end to end, they would reach from Vancouver to St. John's and back to Trois-Rivières, Quebec."

The factoid has great appeal to public relations flacks, politicians, and hog-lazy journalists. For one thing, it usually provides a colourful visual image. (Can't you just picture some bean counter from Statistics Canada carefully laying out a trail of du Mauriers from Vancouver to Newfoundland and halfway back again?)

For another thing, the factoid is almost always original. What other idiot would waste his time converting cigarettes into miles or beer bottles into swimming pools?

But the most delicious attribute of the factoid is that it is virtually uncheckable. You think anybody's going to sit down and *verify* Joe Carter's lifetime at-bats against cud-chewing left-handers? Or how many bottles of Molson's Ex it takes to fill 312 swimming pools? Not likely.

But not impossible, either.

A couple of years ago, a Pittsburgh public relations firm issued a press release claiming that the average American, in the course of a 73.5-year lifetime, spends seven full years in the bathroom.

The *New York Times* duly reported this "statistic." As did the *Wall Street Journal, USA Today,* and who knows how many lesser journals. Only one publication — *Spy Magazine* — said, "Say, what?" and embarked on a little factoid-checking. The folks at *Spy* calculated that the average American would have to spend two hours and twenty minutes in the little room *every day*, seven days a week.

Which is a tad ridiculous. Even for those of us who like to read in there.

Ah, but that's the problem when you start tossing figures around as arguments. Many's the sailor who's drowned in a stream only six inches deep — on average.

Eventually, statistics merely mystify and confuse. The wife of Senator Robert Taft once said, "The only statistic I can remember is that if all the people who go to sleep in church were laid end to end, they would be a lot more comfortable."

Or as Dorothy Parker once wryly observed at a Hollywood party: "If all the girls attending were laid end to end, I wouldn't be surprised."

4

Media Massage

TV or Not TV

We had a real crisis in our house last weekend. There we all were in the family room watching — oh, I forget — *Matlock*, maybe, or a rerun of *The Fugitive* or maybe it was one of those interminable American college football games — the Talahatchee Razor Backs versus the Oshkosh Corn Huskers or something — doesn't matter. Point is, there we were, the whole family gathered around the tube like moths to a sixty-watt bulb when suddenly — PPPPHHHHHHHHHHHT!

The screen went into a series of Picassoesque zigs and zags, flipped three or four times, and faded to an extreme close-up of a blizzard in progress.

TV on the fritz. Happens once in a while. And because it was the weekend, no chance of attracting a repairman before Monday. Instant chorus of murmurations of despair all around the room.

"Swell," groaned our eighteen-year-old. He'd been planning on watching the Movie of the Week.

"Great," sneered our sixteen-year-old. She hasn't missed an episode of *Murder She Wrote* since Jessica Fletcher was in Sleuth School Kindergarten.

I have to confess I was a little ticked off myself. I'd been looking forward to a bowl of popcorn, my feet on the footstool, and spending an hour less commercials with those human pitbulls on *60 Minutes*.

The growling and grumblings went on for a few more seconds, then gradually, inexorably two sets of less-than-voting-age eyes settled on the lord of the manor.

"Well, Dad," said the sixteen-year-old accusingly, "what ARE you supposed to do when you don't have TV? YOU must remember."

Ah yes . . . ask the dinosaur. The only living link between our time

115

and those dark unchannelled ages before David Letterman. What DID we do before TV? I had to think about it.

Then I remembered the Crokinole board — a great plywood octagon that covered most of the dining-room table. I remembered the wooden wafers that you flicked towards the centre of the board, trying to knock out the other players' pieces while getting as close to the bull's-eye as you could. I remembered card games of Euchre and Snap and Fish and board games of Scrabble and Monopoly. I remembered on clear nights lining up to take turns looking through the old brass- and leather-bound telescope that came from Uncle Barney, an ex-sea captain. "That's Orion," my father would say, or, "Look — there's Venus."

I remembered Dickens being read out loud, and sitting entranced around the burnished veneer flanks of a Rogers Majestic upright, staring at the tuning knob, Foster Hewitt's thin and reedy voice ensnaring us all with the feats of Gordie and Reggie and Howie and Teeder.

And I remembered the piano. We never had much money but we did have — incongruously — the piano. And everybody could play at least a little. My sisters knew "Robin in the Rain" and "Kitten on the Keys." My mother specialized in churchly fare like "The Old Rugged Cross" and "Onward Christian Soldiers." And my father could play anything.

Or so it seemed to a ham-fisted pre-television kid. We would gather around the piano and he would launch into "Galway Bay" or "Tennessee Waltz" or "MacNamara's Band." And we would sing! All of us! Off key or on, in time or out. Loudly, flatly, unselfconsciously. Together. And it came to me that we could do it again. Now. On this suddenly, marvellously TV-less night.

"Hey, kids," I yelled, "now listen. We're going to sing 'You Are My Sunshine,' okay? Just like I used to. Except we're going to do it in harmony. It's easy. Dan, you sing YOU ARE MY . . . going down . . . it'll be great! Come on! Count of three!"

But they weren't listening. Or looking. Not at me. The television had flickered back to life.

"Quiet, Dad," they muttered in unison. "*Matlock*'s on."

Music As an
Offensive Weapon

My ancestors, the Scots, have played a goodly number of dirty tricks on civilization.

Haggis. Golf. Scratchy skirts for men.

But the most diabolical trick my forebears ever played has to be that ultimate indignity offered to a sheep's bladder — the bagpipe.

I know about bagpipes. I used to live in the town of Fergus, Ontario — which is about as Scottish as towns get, this side of Hadrian's Wall. Each summer in August, Fergus hosts the Highland Games. That means that each spring in Fergus, the sound of robins and blue jays is drowned out by the caterwauling yowl of pipers warming up, practising for those games.

There are some who will tell you that the sound of the pipes is thrilling, bracing, stirring.

It's always put me in mind of someone in hobnailed boots slowly walking up the spine of an alley cat.

It is a primitive sound, the bagpipe — which is fitting because it's a primitive instrument with an exceedingly narrow range — only nine notes. And six or seven of those sound like they were press ganged into service. It's no accident that Beethoven and Bach never got round to composing for bagpipe — although in later years Beethoven had the prime requirement. He was deaf.

Not surprisingly, war and bagpipes fit together snugly. I'm told that during World War I, German troops were terrified by the sound of skirling pipes coming from the Allied trenches. They knew it was an overture to another attack by kilted Highlanders, whom the Germans called "The Ladies from Hell."

We could have avoided a lot of bloodshed by rendering our Lee

Enfields into drones and chanters. Unleashed wave after wave of bag-pipers on the unsuspecting foe. The war would've been over in weeks.

You know the only saving grace I could discover about the bagpipe? That it's not our fault. We Scots, I mean. The bagpipe is not Scottish. The Scots got it from the Irish. Who probably got it from Celts living in northern Spain, who in turn . . . well, the trail gets a little trampled over the farther back you go. Suffice to say that if you look very closely at certain ancient Sumerian stone tablets, you can make out somebody squeezing a bag under his arm while blowing his brains out.

And you know the old legend about Nero sawing away on a violin while Rome burned? Historians say bunk. For one thing, there were no violins in Nero's time. Nope, historians now figure Nero wasn't fid-dling . . . he was huffing and squeezing. Bagpipes. Was he any good? Well, I think when your audience torches the venue, it's not exactly a standing ovation, but then the sound of bagpipes can make you do strange things.

Astoundingly, the bagpipe is becoming more, not less, popular. And not just in Fergus. There's an American named Rufus something who shows up a couple of times a year in the clubs across Canada playing jazz . . . bagpipe. Czechoslovakia has an entire annual festival devoted to the instrument. And at Carnegie Mellon University in Pittsburgh, it is now possible to take your major in bagpipe.

Obviously, it's a trend and I'm out of step. The bagpipe's coming back. A smart investor would pick this moment in time to put his money where it would do him the most good.

Naw, not in tapes or CDs or bagpipe music.

Not in bagpipe stock even.

I'm sinking my dough into earplug futures.

Life After Muzak? Sorry . . .

Here's a joyous little nugget of news that should help you hum your way through the mid-winter blahs . . . the experts predict that "elevator music" is on its last syrupy refrain. You know the kind of music I mean. The goop you hear in dentists' offices and airport coffee shops. The stuff that leaks out into your ear when the receptionist puts you on hold. "Easy Listening," some folks call it. Background music, a.k.a. Muzak.

The McDonaldization of music, if truth be known.

Easy Listening is heavy on Percy Faith and Mantovani and Barry Manilow — bland and inoffensive ear fodder that can start out as the most inspiring piece of music and wind up as aural porridge. I thought some kind of cultural milestone (or maybe that's millstone) had been reached when I heard the Muzak version of Bob Dylan's Masters of War . . . but I was wrong. It just proved that the Easy Listening engineers could homogenize anything.

But not for much longer, it would seem. Private radio stations in the U.S. are retreating in droves from the Easy Listening format. Of the nearly 10,000 stations across the U.S., only 175 still cling to the Valium sound.

To be replaced by what? Oscar Peterson? k. d. lang? Moe Koffman? Loreena McKennitt? The McGarrigle Sisters? Dream on. Easy Listening may come and Easy Listening may go, but chickens will always need music to lay by and dentists will always need music to drill by.

The new format most radio stations are opting for is called "the Soft Sound" — gonad-less balladeering by the likes of Gloria Estefan, Michael Bolton, Whitney Houston — and, say, where's Mitch Miller when you need him?

What's the difference exactly between Easy Listening music and Soft Sound music? Between Mantovani and Milli Vanilli? Don't ask this tin ear. It all sounds like low-end migraine material to me.

I take comfort in the words of a fellow musical curmudgeon by the name of William Vaughan, who wrote:

"Either heaven or hell will have continuous background music. Which one you think it will be tells a lot about you."

Hit 'Em with Beethoven — Both Barrels

How's the old Shakespearean saw go? "Music hath charms to soothe the savage beast."

Wrong. Shakespeare didn't say it. The playwright William Congreve did. And he didn't say "beast," either — he said "breast." Music hath charms to soothe the savage "breast."

Still, it's an honest mistake we've been memorizing and perpetuating in English classes lo these many years. Honest because history is speckled with attempts by man to use music to calm down, placate, and otherwise distract his fellow terrestrial tenants. There was the Pied Piper, who tootled a nifty flute solo to lead a conga line of rodents out of Hamelin. There are Indian snake charmers who do choreography for their pet cobras. Old MacDonald has found the beat, too. Barns are wired for sound now, providing music for everything from chickens laying eggs to farmers milking cows. Then, of course, there's music to soothe the savage *human* breast. Gondolier sonatas for courting lovers. Strauss waltzes for ice skaters. Mariachi bands for Mexican mooners.

And the public address system at Beaver Hills House Park in downtown Edmonton. Park officials there have rewritten the William Congreve cliché. According to them, it reads: Music hath charms to repel the savage beast.

You see, Beaver Hills House Park had a problem. There it was in the middle of a big, brash city . . . a pleasant oasis of green in a sea of concrete . . . readily available to salve the nerves and soothe the sensibilities of downtown Edmonton office workers . . . except for one thing. The park was full of drug dealers. Great place to go if you wanted to score some crack. Not so great if you were just an ordinary working stiff looking for a little urban relief.

The Edmonton police knew this and they kept an eye on things. But you can't seal off a park. So . . . standoff: how to lose the riffraff without resorting to Nazi tactics.

Answer: music. But unlike the Pied Piper who led the rats out of town, the folks at Beaver Hills House Park *drove* the rats out. They used the park's public address system to play Tchaikovsky Overtures. Albinoni Adagios. Mozart Sonatas. Bach Cantatas. It drives the drug-heads bananas. Not to mention out of the park. Nice to see a social backlash untangled without resorting to barbaric solutions like police batons or Muzak.

But then one shouldn't underestimate the power of music. Even great music. The story is told of the Duke of Wellington sitting through a live performance of Beethoven's homage to the Duke. A work called "Wellington's Victory." Now perhaps the Duke had stood too close to too many cannons but he was not a music lover. Nor was he mealy-mouthed about it. When asked after the performance if the music had captured the glory of the battle, the Duke growled, "By God, no. If it had been that bad I'd have run myself!"

How to Get
Ahead(line)

*Accuracy is to a newspaper what virtue is to a lady, but a
newspaper can always print a retraction.*

ADLAI STEVENSON

Ah, newspapers. History as fishwrap, their critics call 'em, but I
love the imperfect little beggars. For me, newspapers do far more than
deliver the news. They give me pleasure, leisure, provocation, and,
every once in a while, a belly chuckle or two.

And I don't mean the comics.

Some of the best wits I know toil in the bowels of dailies and week-
lies across Canada. Some of the biggest bozos, too. It makes for a heady
and unpredictable brew. It also makes for a lot of humour, much of it
unintentional.

Not that it's an exclusively Canadian phenomenon. Back in the days
when doughty little Britain was a major international player and the
European Common Market had never been dreamed of, the newspapers of the Island Kingdom were famous for their, umm, insularity. As
typified by the headline that appeared in a London daily following
a blizzard: **HUGE STORM. CONTINENT CUT OFF.**

Then there was the parochial approach used by an Aberdeen newspaper to report the sinking of the *Titanic*. The Scottish headline read:
ABERDEEN MAN LOST AT SEA.

But those are laughs at the expense of the newspapers. I enjoy it
even more when a headline writer or a caption slinger takes a look at
a story or a photo, scratches his or her ink-stained mandible, and
comes up with the perfect typographical summation.

Such as the *New York Times* headline that ran above an article about
timekeepers at male track meets. Over a photograph of a half dozen

123

men earnestly peering at their stopwatches was: **THESE ARE THE SOULS THAT TIME MEN'S TRIES**.

Then there is one fabled headline that I have not been able to verify. I'm not sure I really want to, because it's probably too good to be true. The story goes that Gloria Swanson's New York premiere had to be postponed from a Sunday to the following Monday, because of a flash flood, which crippled the bus and subway systems. The headline that supposedly summed up the situation?

SIC TRANSIT, GLORIA MUNDI

From the glorious to the infamous: this double-barrelled story from the pages of the *Enterprise* of Brockton, Massachusetts. In June, the newspaper ran a story in which it named the male customers who had been arrested in the company of hookers. In August, the *Enterprise* ran an editorial saying that it would continue to publish the names of arrested prostitution customers, despite the fact that one man had just killed himself as a result of having been named in the previous *Enterprise* article.

And the name of the dead man? Sorry, the *Enterprise* has a policy of protecting the identity of citizens who commit suicide . . .

My all-time favourite, albeit somewhat gruesome journalistic zinger appeared in the *Chicago Daily News* in an obituary of Richard Loeb back in 1936. Loeb was a college-kid-turned-convicted-child-killer who, while serving his sentence, made a pass at a fellow inmate. The inmate rebuffed Loeb's advances somewhat brusquely, killing Loeb in the process. The lead sentence in the *Daily News* obituary read: "Richard Loeb, the well-known student of English, yesterday ended a sentence with a proposition."

On a less morbid note, I look forward to the day when this "economic downturn" is over and the Good Times roll again.

Then some Hogtown headline writer can liven up the front page of the *Globe and Mail* with the singing headline:

TO-RON-TO BOOM TO-DAY!

I Read It in the Paper

You know what I love about newspapers? I love the fact that trashy and predictable and Chicken Little hysterical as they are . . . they can still surprise you from time to time.

Case in point — the *Globe and Mail.* In it I once found a story with the headline: **Media Interest Scuttles Nuclear Manager's Speech**.

Now you have to think about a headline like that. Media. Interest. Scuttles. Nuclear Manager's. Speech.

Doncha usually give speeches in the hope of *generating* media interest? Well, not always. Apparently, Ken Talbot, manager of the Bruce nuclear generating station, was to speak to some University of Toronto students, until his bosses at Ontario Hydro got wind that reporters might be covering the speech and ordered Mister Talbot to zip his lip. An Ontario Hydro spokesman explained that the event was "turning into something we didn't expect."

Now for years, Ontario Hydro's been offering company PR people as after-dinner speakers, absolutely free. They'll send a speech maker to your high school, your Rotary Club, your local arena . . . to present Ontario Hydro's point of view, no charge. I guess this means they'll still offer the free speakers . . . but only if they can be sure no one will pay attention.

Another bad PR story comes from Ormstown, Quebec, where Roger Hamon requested permission to plant a new crop. A crop with a proven ability to provide extremely low-cost fibres suitable for the production of paper, textiles, rope, and methane. There was just one tiny bureaucratic obstruction between Mister Hamon and his miracle crop: its name, which is Indian hemp. It is a criminal offence to cultivate Indian hemp in Canada. That's because one variety of hemp is marijuana.

Well, one variety of cereal rye becomes bar whiskey and one variety of mushroom is the peyote button, but they don't ban grain farming or mushroom growing.

Of course, if Mister Hamon merely wanted to plant a product that kills 40,000 Canadians a year and herniates our health care system under a burden of preventable cardiovascular disease and respiratory malfunctions . . . If Mister Hamon had merely wanted a licence to plant tobacco, why, Health and Welfare could rubber stamp that, no problem.

But one last story from the *Globe and Mail* takes us across the pond and out of doors for some healthy deep breathing, with a distinctly Canadian touch. Dogsled races! Three hundred and fifty indomitable huskies lined up and straining at the leads on the outskirts of Kielder Forest in northern England. The whines and yips of dogs eager to plunge down the trail . . . the firm commands of fur-clad drivers quieting their teams . . . Don't you wish you could have been there for Britain's first-ever dogsled championship?

Well, actually you probably still can. It was supposed to happen a couple of winters ago, but it's been postponed. They had this big snowstorm you see, and the British officials felt the race might be too dangerous for the dogs . . .

X-Rated Zoodles

I'm sitting here with a tin can of X-rated soup noodles in my hand.

The label reads: "LIBBY'S ZOODLES! NOODLE ANIMALS IN TOMATO SAUCE."

I haven't opened the can yet, but the label leads me to believe it's chock full of slimy little pasta kangaroos, lions, zebras, gorillas, and bears — the better to get the wee ones to eat their lunch, right?

Not according to a forty-two-year-old mother in Glace Bay, Nova Scotia. She says the Zoodles can is the grocery store equivalent of the Penthouse Centrefold. It's gross. It's perverted. It's pornographic.

The hawkeyed Glace Bay housewife insists that when she turns the can upside down, she can clearly see male genitalia hanging down from the elephant on the label — and also in a palm tree in the background.

I say that anybody who spends their leisure time turning cans of noodles upside down looking for genitalia in elephants and palm trees is a citizen in serious need of a hobby, but let that pass. She swears it's there. "If I want to see soft-core pornography," sniffs the housewife, "I think I can go to an adult bookstore and get it."

Easy for her to say, she's probably rich. Have you priced the merchandise at the adult bookstores lately? Outrageous! A can of Zoodles is a lot cheaper. Needless to say, as soon as I heard of the controversy, I streaked to my corner store, bought a can of the unexpurgated noodles, asked to have it wrapped in plain brown paper, and galloped back to my house to be corrupted.

I've been looking for the naughty bits ever since.

What we have here is not an exposé of Adults Only Pasta, it's a resurgence of one of the great crazes of the late twentieth century: subliminal sex in advertising.

It all started more than twenty years ago, when a professor at the University of Western Ontario by the name of Wilson Bryant Key gained international fame. Key claimed that advertisers were secretly brainwashing us by inserting smutty pictures in their work to make us buy their products.

Key asserted that every Ritz cracker had the word SEX embedded on it twelve times on each side. He discerned bare-breasted maidens in the ice blues of liquor advertisements and wrote that once at a fast food restaurant, he'd felt compelled to order fried clams, even though he doesn't like them. While mopping clam juice off his chin, Key says he looked down and discovered the reason for his clam mania — his placemat showed a picture of fried clams, but if you looked *really, really* closely, you could see an orgy going on with images of oral sex and bestiality with a donkey.

Uh huh.

Looney Tunes or not, Key's idea upset a nervous public. Subliminal advertising was banned. Sales of Ritz Crackers and fried clams enjoyed a momentary upsurge.

But only momentary. Because subliminal advertising has one annoying flaw: It doesn't work.

Our own Canadian Broadcasting Corporation proved it in an experiment back in 1958. The CBC announced that "a subliminal message" would be broadcast across the nation during a specific program. Viewers were even told to be on the alert for it! During the program, the message "telephone now" was flashed 353 times in a thirty-minute period.

Nobody phoned.

On the other hand, in the following weeks the CBC received thousands of letters from viewers insisting they had felt unaccountable urges to get up, go for a walk, get a bottle of beer, go to the bathroom — no one guessed the correct message.

Viewers were receptive; the message just wasn't getting through.

And that was a straightforward message. How does Mister Key or the Glace Bay housewife figure a hidden drawing of an elephant's wing-wang is going to propel me to buy Libby's Zoodles by the case?

I've even got a prize for the reader with the best answer.

It's a can of Libby's Zoodles. Well-palmed, but never opened.

Biotrashing

There's a book out about one of my comedy heroes called *The Great One: The Life and Legend of Jackie Gleason*. It's written by a *Time* magazine critic with the near-monarchical name of William A. Henry III.

I won't be reading it.

I won't be reading it because I know too much of what's between the covers already. Thanks to book reviews in the *Globe and Mail* and various news magazines, I'm already aware that Mister Henry's book reveals that Jackie Gleason was:

A drunk.

A bully.

And a slob.

According to the book, even Gleason's grasp of comedy was limited. It claims he was a lousy stand-up comic and a frequently awful actor.

The only thing he was good at was "sketch" comedy — such as Ralph Kramden, the klutzy, bulbous, buffoonish bus-driving schlemiel in *The Honeymooners*.

But as Ralph Kramden, Jackie Gleason was in a class by himself.

Which is why I won't be buying the book. Because that's the Jackie Gleason I knew and loved and wish to remember — as Ralph Kramden. I don't really care to meet the other Not So Great One who screamed at his colleagues, tyrannized writers, and drank like a thirst-crazed camel.

I know enough of those creeps in real life.

And anyway, I'm getting weary of these "clay foot" books — the ones that take as their theme "so you think Joe Bloggs is heroic, eh? Well, here's the real dirt."

I have no problem with books that tell the truth about people. What bugs me are books that set out to deliberately trash their subject, with no pretence of objectivity or even elementary fairness.

In the last while we've seen such books disembowel Nancy Reagan, Chuck and Di, Frank Sinatra, and a pantheon of lesser luminaries too numerous to mention.

Back a few years ago, I made the mistake of reading the very worst of the genre — a best-selling piece of poison penmanship called *Elvis: The Last 24 Hours* by Albert Goldman.

I don't know what Elvis ever did to Albert Goldman, but it must have been pretty nasty, because when it came to demolishing the myths surrounding the King of Rock and Roll, Goldman's book left no sewer tile unturned.

He details every illegal pill and potion Presley popped. Goldman gloated over Presley's abuse of colleagues, his grotesque diet, his weight problems, and his often awful stage performances.

Make no mistake about it — Elvis Aaron Presley was several light-years shy of St. Francis of Assisi. We are talking about a semi-literate, redneck Tennessee truck driver who became, virtually overnight, the most famous human being on the planet. A career move like that can do powerful things to your head.

But the Elvis Goldman describes is some kind of subhuman monster, a greasy-haired, foul-mouthed, swollen-bellied mutant who comes on like an amalgam of Dracula, Don Cherry, and *Predator III*.

Is there anything good that could be said about Elvis Presley? You won't find it in Albert Goldman's book.

Which is what makes Albert Goldman's book a piece of crap. No one is THAT unrelievedly bad. Goldman's grinding a large and ugly axe. You can hear his heavy breathing on every page.

Elvis was definitely a bit of a creep. But he sure could rock and roll. I'd rather listen to his music than sniff his dirty linen.

And Jackie Gleason? When I was a kid, Ralph Kramden made me laugh till I cried. I still catch the odd *Honeymooners* rerun on late-night TV. They still make me laugh, nearly forty years later.

I'm sure they'll be making me laugh long after *The Great One: The Life and Legend of Jackie Gleason* is just a dusty leftover in the Coles remainder bin.

Restricted Reading

Why doesn't somebody invent a birth control pill for magazines?

Have you been past a magazine stand lately? No wonder our forests are threatened. We've got magazines for women and magazines for men and magazines for children. We also have magazines for left-handed hunters, near-sighted car mechanics, pansexual computer nerds, overweight home repair persons, and club-footed skateboarders whose middle initial is "W."

We have so many different magazines these days that it's a challenge to imagine a title for a new one. An American humorist by the name of Robert Byrne gave it a shot a couple of years ago. He came up with:

Gimme! The Magazine of Money

Poor Housekeeping (Ten times the circulation of *Good Housekeeping.*)

And my favourite — *The Shining (formerly Bald World).*

I guess there are a few magazine possibilities still floating around. Now that Dan Quayle's finally given up running for Prez, he's got a little more time on his hands. He might go into publishing. He could sign up Millie, the ex-White House mutt, as a consultant for his first magazine venture — a yearly magazine for dogs.

He could call it *Daniel's Annual Spaniel Manual.*

But kidding aside, there is a new magazine out there that not even Robert Byrne could have dreamed up.

It's called *Prison Life.*

It's strictly for folks who are involuntary guests of the U.S. penitentiary system.

Sounds like another joke, until you think about the numbers. There are more than a million convicts in state and federal prisons across the

United States. There are another 3 million on probation or parole. What's more, the numbers are expanding because criminals are a growth industry. The U.S. prison roll call jumps by about 7 percent each year.

So what kind of articles would you find in *Prison Life*? Well, what sort of things would you want to read about if you were doing seven-to-ten? There's a regular column called "The Chaplain Speaks" and another called "Ask The Law Professor." There's even a feature entitled "In-Cell Cooking."

Not that *Prison Life* is just a kind of *Chatelaine*-with-Stripes. Its first issue featured America's least-favourite Lifer on the cover under a headline that read: CHARLIE MANSON: GET OFF HIS BACK!

Then, too, there's the *Prison Life* centrefold — a fetching young thing in a wisp of bikini smiling back at the reader. This is the "Cellmate of the Month" — and since there are several hundred thousand women in the slammer, the Cellmate comes in both male and female varieties.

But the factor that makes or breaks a magazine is the advertising it can attract — and who's going to advertise in a magazine for felons?

Well, true — you won't find many Chase-Manhattan or Yale Lock ads in *Prison Life*, but you'd be surprised who has lined up to buy space. There's a full-page spread for health food supplements (a lot of cons get into weightlifting and body-building). There's even an ad paid for by Island Records flogging a new Tom Waits album.

When you think of it, a magazine for convicts isn't a dumb idea at all. Prisoners just may be the last untapped consumer market on the continent.

And unlike the old days, the new cons have lots of pocket money. In the U.S. they can earn up to $2,000 a year.

Doesn't sound like much, but don't forget — food, board, and the company uniform are supplied free of charge.

Plus, inmates have one precious freedom when it comes to magazines that you and I will never know.

Plenty of time to read the damn things.

Lost in the Translation

Is it me — or is Life really full of dirty tricks?

Back in 1963, I felt privileged to have witnessed (if only via my seventeen-inch Admiral TV) one of the great oratorical moments in history. It happened in Berlin. A young, tousle-haired American president by the name of John Fitzgerald Kennedy faced an enthusiastic crowd of West Germans and declared, "Ich bin ein Berliner!"

Well, that wasn't too hard to follow. JFK was telling his German allies that as long as the Berlin Wall stood, he would be, in spirit, a citizen of Berlin, right?

Wrong.

Turns out that in Germany a "Berliner" is kind of like a bagel or a turnover, only with jam inside.

So what Kennedy was declaring on that cold, grey day in Berlin thirty-odd years ago was:

"I am a jelly doughnut."

Well, Lord knows it's not the only international misunderstanding in history — even for U.S. presidents. Back in 1977, Jimmy Carter caused a few red faces during a visit to Poland thanks to a Not Terribly Good translator who announced that the U.S. president had "abandoned" the United States. (He meant that Carter had "left" the U.S. that day.)

The hapless translator also had poor Jimmy talking about Polish "lusts." (Carter had merely been speculating on the people's "desires for the future.")

But translation is a tricky game. I have in my library a classic piece of inter-lingual butchery written by one Pedro Carolino back in 1883. It's called *The New Guide of Conversation in Portuguese and English.*

Right from the title you know this is no ordinary foreign phrase book. Consider Senhor Carolino's dedication:

"We expect then, who the little book (for the care what we wrote him, and for her typographical correction) that may be worth the acceptation of the studious persons, and especially of the youth, at which we dedicate him particularly."

My favourite section is the one with instructions on how to get your money back for a lousy horse:

"Here is a horse who have bad looks. Give me another. I will not that. He not sall know to march, he is pursy, he is foundered. Don't you are ashamed to give me a jade as like? He is undshoed. He is with nails up."

Scientific experts can screw up, too. As the folks in charge of a museum in northern England did a few years back, when they proudly exhibited a Roman *sestertium* coin, minted, they said, more than 1,800 years ago.

Quite popular it was, too, until a little nine-year-old girl came along and piped: "That's not a Roman coin. It's a plastic thing you get from Robinson's Soft Drinks."

The little girl was absolutely right. As a public relations campaign, a local soft drinks firm had been handing out plastic tokens in exchange for bottle labels.

A red-faced museum curator explained that the museum experts had been taken in by the big letter "R" on the coin. "The trouble was that we construed the letter to stand for 'Roma.' In fact, it stood for 'Robinson's,' the soft drink manufacturers."

Not that newspapers are immune to the disease. First prize for the all time worst newspaper reporting must surely go to the *Wiltshire Times and Chippenham News* for a feature article it ran about a local man named Harris.

The following week, the paper carried this apology.

"Mr. Harris has asked us to point out a number of inaccuracies in our story. After returning from India, he served in Ireland for four years and not six months as stated; he never farmed at Heddington, particularly not at Coate Road Farm as stated; he has never counted cycling or walking among his hobbies; he is not a member of 54 hunts; and he did not have an eye removed at Chippenham Hospital after an air raid on Calne."

Oh well. At least they spelled his name right.

Mighty Blighty
Gets Up-Tighty

Canada is a vast expanse of land where the inhabitants drink beer, watch hockey and are so square even the female impersonators are women.

SUNDAY TIMES MAGAZINE *JULY 4, 1993*

Oh dear. The Brits are at it again. I don't know if it's their wretched climate, their inedible cuisine, or just a consequence of being trapped in a clapped-out, ninth-rate, fading Used-To-Be United Kingdom, but the British press always seems to have lots of cheap shots to lob at Canada. The latest tirade in London's *Sunday Times* rants on for three pages about how boring and buffoonish our country is.

I think the author, one Simon Mills, must have done most of his creative work over large mugs of Watney's Red Barrel down at the local pub, because the article is confusing and incoherent, even for a rant. Quite aside from misspelling the name of a Margaret Atwood bestseller, the whole item is speckled with bizarre sentences such as: "The inhabitants like ice hockey and drink beer and the Monty Python lot used to dress up as Mounties."

Sounds like the author thinks John Cleese and pals were Canucks.

I wish it were so, but sorry chaps, the Pythoners were ah . . . British.

The article then goes on to snipe at various famous Canadians. Michael J. Fox is "vertically challenged." Boy, that's original. Rocker Bryan Adams is snickered at for having a hit song in the number one slot of the U.K. Hit Parade for sixteen weeks.

This is a bad thing?

Canadian model Linda Evangelista is mocked and derided because she once said she wouldn't even get out of bed for less than $10,000.

"Which," a breathless author Mills informs us, "presuming she was talking Canadian dollars, is only about $8,000 in 'real' money."

The whole article is like that — goofy, lame, and off the mark. Lord knows there's plenty to spoof about Canada, but you won't find it in the pages of the *Sunday Times Magazine*.

And it ill behooves a nation that gave the world Neville Chamberlain, bangers and mash, and Twiggy to start calling any other nation dull.

This isn't the first time outsiders have held their noses and sniffed disdainfully over the shortcomings of the Great White North. Away back in the eighteenth century, the French philosopher Voltaire dismissed Canada as "a few acres of snow." Al Capone snarled, "I don't even know what street Canada is on." In Parisian argot, "un Canada" used to mean a bad apple. In Spanish slang, when somebody wants to say, "He's in jail," they smirk and murmur, "Esta en Canada."

But you know what I notice? I notice that there are not immense lineups down at Canada Customs full of Canucks itching to go and live in Madrid or Versailles or Middlesex or Stoke on Trent.

Quite the contrary. The traffic seems to be all in the other direction. Spaniards and Portuguese and French and — my goodness! — British as well, giving up their pasts to come and make a life in chilly old, boring old, provincial Canada.

Why is that, do you reckon? Could we, in all our squareness, be doing something right?

Could it be that, when all is said and done, Canada is still "the Golden Mountain" as the first Chinese who arrived in British Columbia described it, a century and a quarter ago?

Could it be that to be rich, successful, and in the gravy is, as the Polish expression has it, "to have Canada?"

Nah, it couldn't be.

Otherwise the British press would surely have told us.

Student Bloopers

Not long ago, *Rolling Stone* magazine performed a public service. It published a list of American college courses currently available, that, as the magazine phrased it "even your dog could pass." Students at a Texas university could enroll in a credit course called The History of Rock Music. Cornell University offers Supervised Reading. Students at Pepperdine are signing up for Surfing. At Northwestern University it is possible to earn a credit by passing a course called Choosing a Life.

I'm not making mock here. I'm merely suggesting that it may be no accident that North American students habitually place last whenever they compete in international student quizzes. It shouldn't be surprising really. The West German school year is a full two months longer than the North American one. Saturday is a school day in Japan and Korea. On the other hand, the average Canadian or American student spends about 900 hours a year in class — and another 1,170 hours sitting in front of the boob tube.

I'm still not going on a rant about this. I merely offer it as a possible explanation for the kind of results Richard Lederer has been noticing.

Mister Lederer taught English at St. Paul's School in Concord, New Hampshire, for more than a quarter of a century. During that time he came across so many student bloopers in essays and test papers that he began to collect them. Having collected them, he decided to share them with the nonacademic world in a book called *Anguished English*.

What sort of student bloopers? Here's a cluster plucked from the work of four different would-be scholars on the subject of love and marriage:

"Having one wife is called monotony."

"A man who marries twice commits bigotry."

"When a man has more than one wife he is a pigamist."

"Acrimony is what a man gives his divorced wife."

Lederer's students weren't a lot better when they applied their talents to other academic disciplines. A biology student wrote: "There are three kinds of blood vessels: arteries, vanes and caterpillars."

A would-be anthropologist explained: "A fossil is an extinct animal. The older it is, the more extinct it is."

And a youngster who almost certainly won't cop the Nobel Prize for Chemistry insisted, "H2O is hot water and CO2 is cold water . . ."

Ah, but it's the student historians who really steal the show in Richard Lederer's blooper collection. Listen to one of them give a thumbnail sketch of Egypt:

"The inhabitants of Egypt were called mummies. They lived in the Sarah Dessert and travelled by Camelot. The climate of the Sarah is such that the inhabitants have to live elsewhere, so certain areas of the dessert are cultivated by irritation. The Egyptians built Pyramids in the shape of a huge triangular cube. The Pyramids are a range of mountains between France and Spain."

Their grasp of Ancient Greece and Rome was similarly shaky:

"Without the Greeks, we wouldn't have history. The Greeks invented three kinds of columns Corinthian, Doric and Ironic. They also had myths. A myth is a female moth. One myth says that the mother of Achilles dipped him in the River Stynx until he became intolerable. Achilles appears in "The Iliad" by Homer. Homer also wrote the "Oddity" in which Penelope was the last hardship that Ulysses endured on his journey. Actually, Homer was not written by Homer but by another man of that name."

Nor did their grasp of the Renaissance seem quite complete. "It was an age of great inventions and discoveries," wrote one student. "Gutenberg invented the Bible. Sir Walter Raleigh invented cigarettes. Another important invention was the circulation of blood. Sir Francis Drake circumcised the world with a 100-foot clipper."

Ouch.

5

Destination: Anybody's Guess

Frankenstein Travel Tales

Do you have a travel horror story? Of course you do. Travel these days is fraught with gut-curdling terror, breathtaking incompetence, and soaring churlishness. Any mortal who has passed through the bowels of Pearson International airport, the front door of the Buffalo Bus Terminal, or the backseat of a Montreal taxi has at least one travel horror story.

You want to share your travel horror story with the world? Go write your own book. This one's mine, and here is my tale of tourist trauma.

It happened in the Bahamas. A large national airline, which shall remain nameless, sent me two free airline tickets and a reservation at a plush spa called . . . I forget — Paradise or Ambrosia or Nirvana or something like that. "Go," they told me. "Take your wife. Enjoy yourself. Write something nice about it for our magazine."

Well, it sure sounded better than staying in Canada shovelling out my driveway. We dropped our mittens, threw a couple of tubes of Coppertone in a bag, and headed for the airport.

I won't gross you out with all the details but they include getting lost in the Atlanta airport, flying over the Bermuda Triangle in a single engine plane with a pilot whose breath smelled of aftershave, arriving at a hotel that had never heard of me or the aforementioned large national airline, getting a flat tire on the plane taking us to Nassau, being in a taxi whose driver's sole acquaintance with English was the phrase, "No, mon," and, finally, having a villa in the hills that featured absolutely everything.

Except electricity.

The low point of the trip came when I found myself negotiating through a closed door with what I thought was an unusually shrewish concierge.

"Do you have a reservation for Arthur Black?" I asked the door. From the other side came a cackling command, "COME IN! COME IN!"

"Ah, I can't come in, ma'am . . . the door appears to be locked. Do you ha — "

"COME IN! COME IN!"

This conversation went on for several sweaty minutes until suddenly the concierge squawked and I realized I'd been engaged in conversation with a blue-fronted Amazon parrot.

Back home, I wrote a true story about our Bahamas vacation. The large national airline declined to print it in their magazine. "We don't handle X-rated material," they explained.

That's my travel horror story, but it's a Disney cartoon next to Robert Banting's tale of woe. Banting was rushing out to catch a night flight from Toronto to Montreal. His cab skidded off the exit ramp and crashed. Emerging unhurt from the wreckage, Banting fished out his bags and hailed another cab, which got him to the airport just in time to coincide with a phoned-in bomb threat for his flight. Several hours of Mounties, rent-a-cops, and cups of bad coffee later, Banting was hustled onto another plane. Then he was frog-marched off the plane by security officers and taken to his suitcase, which a police dog was sniffing suspiciously. "Open it," they commanded. He did. The dog lunged for the roast beef sandwich Banting had packed.

Banting got to his Montreal hotel just as dawn was creeping across the sky. Naturally his reservation had been cancelled. And, of course, his luggage was by now on its way to Halifax.

The good news is that Robert Banting's trial by travel earned him the Frankenstein Travel Award. It's a prize given out annually by the Executive Communications Group of New Jersey, for the most horrendous travel story of the year.

They must have mailed the award to Banting. He sure as hell didn't fly to New Jersey to pick it up.

Eating on the Fly

I think I've come up with a new oxymoron. You know oxymorons? An oxymoron is when two contradictory words join together to form a figure of speech. Jumbo shrimp is an oxymoron. So is bitter sweet. And deafening silence. And Military Intelligence. And Civil Service. And Progressive Conservative (remember them?).

Anyway, I think I've discovered a new oxymoron. My nomination is Airline Food.

I flew back from Halifax on a dinner flight last week. I know it was a dinner flight because I can see the tinfoil cuts on my hands and I still have the heartburn.

But I have no idea what I ate. The flight attendant asked me if I wanted the chicken or the salmon and I said "chicken," but there must have been another option behind door number three, because what he put in front of me was neither fish nor fowl, nor animal nor veg-etable nor mineral nor necessarily of this solar system.

Pretty. It was quite pretty. Good colour composition with the russets of the meat-like substance neatly complimenting the ash-grey of the ersatz potato. Great texture too . . . a side order of pale green gravel that could have passed for a Grandma Moses' rendition of garden peas. Old garden peas. And the dessert? The dessert was . . . some-thing else. Abstract. Postmodernist, maybe. And anyway, academic because it was sealed under an impermeable barrier of transparent membrane that would have brought sobs of futility to the throat of a safecracker. I didn't try very hard. I knew what it would taste like.

Ever wonder if airline food *has* to be so maddeningly bland? Well, I did some checking and the answer is apparently, yes, it does. It has to do with too many fussy eaters and extremely limited storage space on board and mostly with the sheer volume of meals that have to be prepared each day. One food supplier, Cara Operations, runs flight kitchens in thirteen major airports right across this country. The Halifax kitchen has to turn out 3,500 meals every day — and contrary to what our taste buds report, they are not all the same.

Fly out of Vancouver and you're much more likely to be offered a choice of fish for dinner. Fly out of Calgary, count on beef.

When you think about it, it's pretty miraculous to get anything hot, fresh, and remotely edible considering that you are winging along in a large stainless steel cigar at 350 miles an hour, some 30,000 feet over the Canadian landscape. And by the way, we in Canada are lucky. Canadian Airlines says it spends an average of $10.94 wining and dining each passenger — okay, not wining. They ding you $2.00 a pop for a glass of plonk now. But as I say, we're fortunate. Southwest Airlines in the States lays out a stingy 17 cents per flying customer. Fly Southwest and you will be treated to peanuts, a can of pop, and a complimentary barf bag.

Which for some reason reminds me of the story about the British woman who phoned up her travel agent to ask how long the Concorde took to fly from Heathrow in London to La Guardia in New York. The travel agent, who was juggling two other calls, said, "Ah, just a minute, madame."

"Thank you," said the caller and hung up.

Mind you that wouldn't be a dinner flight.

What I Did on My Vacation

Hey, pal, you had it with the snow shovel and the fur-lined Sorels? Fed up with the daily duel with jumper cables, block heaters, and rock salt for the driveway?

Try this on for size: Tropical island . . . palm trees . . . coconuts at your bare feet . . . a beach hut no more than a frisbee throw from the warm, foamy ocean surf . . . all-you-can-eat meals . . . sun, sand . . . fireball sunsets . . . bonfires on the beach . . . singalongs . . .

And all for fifty bucks a night?

Well, about three-quarters of a night, actually. Three-quarters of a night because at five-thirty every morning a gong will be clanged and you will be encouraged — no, *expected* — to rise and dress and make your way to a concrete floored temple, there to squat cross-legged and meditate silently for two straight hours.

After that you get to spend another two hours stretching your body into configurations you never dreamed a body could configure.

Ah, but by then it's ten in the morning and you get to tuck into one of those all-you-can-eat meals I promised.

That's . . . all you can eat as long as it isn't meat. Or fish. Or eggs. Or coffee. Or alcohol. Or an after-breakfast ciggie.

It's a yoga ashram in the Bahamas I write of and I know what I'm talking about for a change. I spent a week at the place.

Now just about everybody I've mentioned this to has interrupted me at this point with a, "Huh, not for me, man — when I go on vacation I drink margueritas, eat steak and lobster, and sleep in. None of that discipline stuff. I go on holidays to relax."

Well, all I can say is, the vegetarian food I had was delicious and filling . . . I didn't miss the hangovers or the sleep-ins . . . and as for the rigorous discipline — the last time I felt that relaxed, I was wearing blue wool booties and a diaper.

Mind you, there was effort. The yoga exercises are as demanding as you care to make them — but there's no drill sergeant standing over you counting cadences or growling, "No pain, no gain, maggot!" In yoga, you move at your own speed.

And there was discipline. You get to rake. And sweep. And wash pots and pans. You have to attend the meditations and the exercise classes. Don't go and they show you the gate. Without a refund.

Still, I loved it. But then I'm weird. Maybe you better talk to that chubby Québécois with the white hair over there. He's from Montreal. He's only been coming here for the past seventeen years. Or check with that skinny guy, Ed, down by the dock. He's from New Jersey. In the summers, that is. He's spent his past twenty-one winters doing meditations and sun salutations at the ashram.

Would I go again? You bet. Would I recommend it? Well, only if you're ready for, as the Monty Python talking news head says, "something completely different."

But not *scary* different. The Bahamas ashram experience will not steal your mind or turn you into an ululating saffron-robed denizen of airport lounges. But it will change your gears and oil your hinges.

And if you ever did feel your untranscendental North American soul slipping away . . . well, rumour has it that just down the beach from the ashram, there's a restaurant at the Club Med that makes a damn fine cheeseburger and fries for about six bucks and change.

I don't know that for a fact, you understand. It just came to me in a vision, while I was repeating my mantra.

A Glorious Bald Rock

When you grow up as a central Canadian schoolkid, they teach you all sorts of things about Newfoundland. You learn that it's Canada's youngest province, not throwing its sou'wester into the Confederation ring until 1949. You get taught all about Pal Joey and the Merchant Prince Crosbies and the faint, sad dirge of the slaughtered Beothuck Indians. The school texts talk of the wealth of the inland forests, the fecundity of the Grand Banks, the oily promise of Hibernia — or at least they used to. But you do not learn in school the things that a visit to Newfoundland lays out for you to see plainly.

Mostly what they don't teach in class is the sheer physical mass of the place. In the school atlas, Newfoundland was that little pink cluster just off the starboard rail of the continent. Little? The place is bigger than Ireland and a damn sight less manicured. I spent seven days just meandering over the Avalon Peninsula. That's in the southeast corner of the province. A fragment of the whole — a mere knucklebone of rock and trees and outports surrounding the capital, St. John's. Seven days. I didn't even scratch the topsoil.

Mind you, I saw plenty. Carbonear and Salmon Cove and Holyrood and Dunville and Spaniard's Bay and Bay Roberts and Blackhead. And in one ridiculously quixotic afternoon I tiptoed through Heart's Desire, Heart's Delight, and Heart's Content — all of which are no more than a dory ride and a coronary pitty-pat from a hamlet called Little Heart's Ease.

These are not cutesy-poo, calico, and quilted duckling tourist traps we're talking about here. These are hardscrabble, working fishermen's outports. And these are the names that the citizens chose for their hometowns. How could you not love the place?

Magic moments. I asked directions to a gas station in Harbour Grace. Fellow told me it was, "Just over the hill bye — about t'ree gunshots." A gunshot, it turns out, is the distance a muzzle-loading rifle could lob a bullet. Which doesn't really answer the question, does it? When's the last time you hoisted a musket to your shoulder? Still, it's a lot more romantic than, say, half a kilometre — which equally mystifies me.

A linguist could dive into the Newfoundland map and expire from rapture of the deep. What can you say about a kingdom that boasts place names like Famish Gut, Witless Bay, Jigger Tickle, Ireland's Eye, Backside Pond, Horney Head, Nogging Cove, and Sop's Arm?

It's a magical place. Apt to vanish at any moment in a swirl of Merlinesque fog. I saw an Alfa Romeo convertible slogging up a hill in a sleet storm outside New Perlican and thirty seconds later I came upon a cow moose in the middle of the same road and I'm hard-pressed to decide which made less sense.

I saw with my own eyes, huge icebergs, like alabaster galleons, gliding and grinding down the coast. And this in the month of May. Also in the month of May I saw a snowstorm . . . and a flock of warblers . . . and people changing from short-sleeved shirts to duffle coats in the same afternoon, faster than Superman in a phone booth. Ah, the Newfoundland weather. The Rock has turned out its share of statesmen, tycoons, hockey players . . . but few strippers. In Newfoundland the tendency is to put clothes on, not take them off.

Then there's the sheer kindness of the place. When I complimented my bed-and-breakfast hostess on the tastiness of her homemade partridge-berry jam, she saw to it that a jar of same was secreted into my baggage. I told the principal of a rural high school about it the next day, which led to a chat about other island delights, like bake-apples and cloudberries. When I was ready to leave, the principal met me with two frosty jars in his hand — one of bakeapples, the other of cloudberries. He'd run home and pulled them out of his freezer while I was talking to the kids.

You've got to be careful with Newfoundlanders. You compliment them on something and right away they give it to you. That's how I ended up with enough jam to last me till the Second Coming.

Thank God I didn't say anything nice about the cow moose.

Toronto: Not Quite Ready for Prime Time

This is a story about two human settlements. One of them is called Astakos. It's in Greece.

The other one is known as Hogtown, Zurich-On-The-Humber, The Queen's City, Taranna the Good — or just Toronto.

I don't know a whole lot about the settlement called Astakos. It's not listed in my World Atlas, so I figure it's safe to assume that it's smaller than Toronto.

In some ways, at any rate.

As for the other settlement, I know a fair bit about it. I was born there, for one thing. And in the half a century since, I have called it home from time to time. Worked there. Studied there. Got married and divorced and hired and fired and drunk and happy and sad there.

So I have my own hard-earned opinions about Toronto — but then, breathes there a Canuck from the Queen Charlottes to Signal Hill who doesn't? We all know what we think about Ontario's capital. And generally speaking, the farther away you live, the less edifying the sentiments.

It's an easy city to dislike. Toronto doesn't have the easy beauty of Vancouver or the joie de vivre of Montreal. It lacks the architectural grace of Ottawa, the mountainscape backdrop of Calgary, the down-home warmth of St. John's, Winnipeg, or Windsor. To the outsider, Toronto feels fast and brittle and cold and more than a touch arrogant.

Toronto feels like it is about money.

Or perhaps even less. After all, Las Vegas is about money, too, but at least people enjoy themselves there. Torontonians seldom look like they're having a good time. Oh, they fill the seats in Skydome and Maple Leaf Gardens, but visiting sports teams speak with disbelief about the eerie quietness of Toronto fans.

Torontonians don't take easily to new cultural concepts, either. Remember The Archer? It's a sculpture created by the late, great Henry Moore. A vast, shining nugget of burnished bronze that glows and catches the sun in Nathan Phillips Square. Moore wanted so badly to see it standing in front of Toronto's New City Hall that he slashed the price to be a bargain basement $100,000.

Torontonians freaked out.

What is it, they squawked. Looks like a chicken with its head cut off. Can't tell the front from the back. One city councillor grumbled, "How much art and culture . . . can we have shoved down our throats?"

Well, that was more than a quarter of a century ago, and Toronto has more or less grown grudgingly accustomed to that stunning bronze brooch pinned to its bosom. It isn't loved. It just isn't talked about anymore.

Instead they're kvetching about The Rock.

The Rock is a massive slab of Muskoka granite that was installed in a downtown park. Once again Torontonians are bleating about the extravagance of featuring something as unproductive as Precambrian stone when the space could be used to make money — another parking lot, say . . . or maybe a McDonald's.

And if it must be a damned park, then, as city councillor Tom Jacobek imaginatively suggested, "What's wrong with simply laying some sod and planting a few bushes?"

Ah, yes. That's the Toronto we've all come to know and loathe.

Which brings us full circle, to the Greek settlement of Astakos, Greece, that I mentioned way back at the beginning.

Do you know what they do in Astakos?

Every time there's a rainbow in the sky, the city fathers serve free glasses of wine to everybody in the town square.

I don't know how Astakos racks up against Toronto in other respects — garbage pickup, sewers and sidewalks, public transportation . . .

But I know which town I'd rather be having dinner in tonight.

School Daze

The students are used to being entertained. They are used to the idea that if they are just the slightest bit bored, they can flip the switch and turn the channel.

TEACHER QUOTED IN THE NEW YORK TIMES

I was raking the leaves the other day when a neighbour called me over. He handed me a crumpled piece of paper. "What do you make of this?" he asked. A childish ballpoint scrawl limped across the page. It looked like something you might get if you gave a chicken LSD, dipped its feet in an inkwell, and turned it loose on a piece of foolscap. The first three words seemed to read "I ha went" . . . then the note degenerated into indecipherable hieroglyphics.

"I can't make it out," I confessed. "What's it say?"

"Beats me," said my neighbour. "It's a note that Charlie left by the telephone."

Charlie is my neighbour's son. The whole occurrence would be unremarkable if Charlie was seven years old, a victim of Parkinson's disease, or a terminal heroin addict. In fact, he is a resoundingly normal eighteen-year-old. And he graduated from high school last spring.

With excellent marks in English.

How is it possible that a kid can be simultaneously ready for university and unable to write a legible, literate telephone message? I don't know, but I know that Charlie is no isolated case. Most of the teenagers I know can't even talk. Not in sentences. Not without stuffing every chink in their conversation with "y' know's" and "like, ummmm's" and "rilly's."

I know, I know. I sound like a bring-back-the-birch, why-in-my-day, Preston Manning geek. But it isn't just me, folks. Listen to the words of

Sabina Petrecchia. Consider the testimony of Elodie Feltin. Ask Nils Nonner and Kika Schossland.

Who they? Teenagers. Schoolkids. From Italy, Switzerland, Germany, and Brazil, respectively. They spent one school year attending classes as exchange students at a high school in southwestern Ontario.

They couldn't believe what they saw.

Sabina, from Rome, said: "School is very different in Italy. There is no such thing as a spare . . . we do homework from four to five hours every day, not half an hour or an hour like here."

She also points out that Italian students go to school six days a week, spend five years in high school, and take thirteen compulsory (look it up, children) subjects each year — including math, science, Latin, philosophy, and English.

Elodie, who hails from Lausanne: "It's incredible to me that [Canadian] students shout and talk in class. We could never do that in Switzerland. The teachers are much more strict."

And how does she find educational standards in Canada?

A joke. She says Canadian homework assignments are a snap.

Kika Schossland, who normally attends high school in Recife, Brazil, was shocked by the boozing among Canadian high schoolers. "Students here smoke and drink a lot more than in Brazil," she observed. "They [Canadian kids] go to parties and get drunk."

For Nils Nonner, a seventeen-year-old exchange student from Stuttgart, cars were the big eye opener. In Germany, he explained, high school kids driving cars were seen about as often as unicorns. In Stuttgart, students get around on bicycles, public transit, or by foot. Nils couldn't believe the sea of student-driven chrome and rubber surrounding the average Canadian high school.

He has a point. Recently the high school in my home town seriously proposed levelling a mature grove of pine trees and messing up a park to provide still more parking for students.

Parking? For students? Isn't that why we subsidize fleets of school buses?

Twenty-five hundred years ago, the great philosopher Aristotle wrote: "The fate of empires depends on the education of the young."

If that's so, then heaven help the empire of Canada.

The Game of Golf: Now and Zen

I have to tell you, I had hope for the Japanese. I really did. Few cultures in the history of civilization were handed the opportunity Japan was. World War II saw to that. Thanks to Harry Truman and the last most famous flight of a lumpy old B29 named the *Enola Gay*, Japan had the chance, after several years of cultural agglomeration, to quite simply wipe the slate clean and start all over again. In 1945 after Nagasaki and Hiroshima, Japan was a clean blackboard, a blank computer screen, capable of anything. And what did the Japanese do with this once-in-a-millennium opportunity?

They discovered golf.

Well, sure. Haven't you heard? The Japanese are golf nuts. High-powered business executives put their names on lists and pay tens of thousands of dollars for the privilege of teeing off into the smog at three in the morning on the lip of some gravel pit on the outskirts of Yokohama.

They join high-rise golf clubs — featuring courses that go up, not out. Duffers shooting off the green on the fourth hole aim their shots up a storey, then catch an elevator to play the next hole.

Hey, the Japanese are so serious about golf that they've even entered the annals of Golf Folklore.

You haven't heard about the near-mortal hole in one — in which a Tokyo golfer stroked a beautiful 220 yard riser that went straight down the fairway, whacked a fellow golfer in the forehead, knocked him cold *but* still dribbled into the cup for a hole in one?

Good, but not as good as the shot by Iokai Mitsiko, who stroked a powerful drive off the third green on a golf course in Kyoto last summer, a drive that soared up . . . then down . . . then onto a pond . . .

then, incredibly, ACROSS the pond . . . up, off a small oak tree, rico-cheting off another oak tree onto the green, and into the cup for a hole in one. "I thought I was seeing things," said the golfer Mitsiko. "The ball had enough spin to skid across the surface of the pond, then it bounced off the trees like a pinball machine, onto the green and into the hole."

Well, pretty good . . . almost as good as the story of the time Moses asked God if he was up for a round of golf. God said sure. They met next day at their favourite course, flipped a loonie, and Moses got to tee off.

Moses hit a pretty decent drive . . . 275 yards straight down the fair-way. Good shape for the green.

Then God steps up . . . squares off . . . squints down the fairway . . . winds up . . . hits a . . . pathetic blooper that wobbles up, wavers to the right . . . fades down, down into the deep bush overhanging a swamp . . . bounce, bounce, plop. Into the ooze. But suddenly, the ball sur-faces again, on the back of a turtle . . . the turtle starts swimming for shore, whereupon a huge golden eagle appears out of nowhere, swoops like a dive bomber, grabs God's Spalding in its talons . . . starts pumping its wings and climbing . . . five hundred feet, eight hundred feet . . . a thousand feet . . . fifteen hundred feet . . . barrel rolls and releases the ball so that it falls down, down, down, down right in the centre of a small lake . . . splash, the ball hits the surface, whereupon suddenly a giant trout lunges to the surface of the lake, turns on its side, cups the golf ball on its powerful tail and FLIPS the ball over the shore past a sand trap and right up onto the green. The ball dribbles straight for the cup . . . and kerflop. A hole in one.

Back on the green, Moses turns to God and snarls:

"We gonna play some golf today — or are you just gonna fool around?"

That's a joke that so far just doesn't translate into Japanese.

That New Time Religion

I'm a sinner. A backslider. A non-churchgoer.

Wasn't raised that way, though. My folks made sure I was sitting, scrub-faced and twitchy, third pew from the front in St. Andrew's Presbyterian Church every Sunday. Sat there till I got too big to tackle.

And I've tried churchgoing a few times since then. Caught the Christmas service in Westminster Abbey one year. And passed a few sultry Spanish afternoons (not always Sundays) within the cool dank walls of some fine, old Catholic churches in Madrid and Barcelona. But my attempts at ecclesiastical grafting never took, somehow. Never got the pang of piety. Always felt in church the way I do when I see a polished parquet floor with a dance band warming up on the other side. Which is to say, bewildered and a little bit intimidated and ever so slightly on the wrong planet.

Always thought the old curmudgeon H. L. Mencken had a pretty good take on churches. "Church," said H. L., "is a place in which gentlemen who have never been to Heaven brag about it to people who will never get there."

Church is not my cup of tea, but it used to be something I was at least wary of. When an institution tells you you're going to burn eternally in Hell if you don't do things its way, you have to at least . . . *nod* in its direction. The Church used to have my grudging respect, but less so, of late.

And it's not just the Mount Cashels and the Swaggarts and the Oral Robertses. It's things like . . . well, the Church of England just issued a slick Much Music–style video aimed at enticing British youth into the Christian fold. This video features guitars, lite rock music, kids schmoozing at a religious rally, the Archbishop of Canterbury wearing a baseball cap, and even a bishop rapping with a Jewish rabbi and a Muslim Imam. Goes on for half an hour, this Christian promotional video. Doesn't once mention Christ.

When asked about that, the Church of England's communications officer sniffed, "It's not that kind of video."

Not that we need to cross the Atlantic to find an example of Church wussiness in action. Take the case of Christopher Bowen versus the Montreal Presbytery of the United Church of Canada. They had a falling out because Mister Bowen appeared as a kind of a feature in an Ottawa-based magazine called *Malebox*. In most of the photos, Mister Bowen wasn't wearing a clerical collar. Or anything else.

Nor was this his first foray into magazine modelling. He appeared as Mister November in a calendar called Forge 1993 Leather.

Are we quibbling here about Mister November's right to pose starkers for a hard-core porn mag? Absolutely not. This is a free society. People can earn $4 million a year throwing baseballs or even sleep on steam grates if they like. Mister Bowen has a constitutional right to be Mister November in the Forge Leather calendar.

We just wonder if he should do it while he's also pastor of the Roxboro United Church, that's all.

Apparently the United Church of Canada wondered, too. After much dithering, they voted — not to chastise the minister, mind, or criticize his extra-curricular activities. But to temporarily suspend him. And to keep the whole thing out of the papers.

Fat chance. The story broke wide open when the Reverend Bowen elected to sue the Church for wrongful dismissal.

And the Church's reaction? Wellsir, the Church is hurt. Hurt and upset. But the Church insists this is not a disciplinary matter. Merely one of . . . inappropriate behaviour. Which is why they suspended the vicar . . . but with full pay.

The whole story has a plaintive, forlorn undertone. Reminds me of the wistful observation: "Every day more people are straying away from the Church . . . and going back to God."

I didn't make that up. Came from another old sinner. Name of Lenny Bruce.

Members of the Club

You want a weird word? I'll give you a weird word: club.

Club. Sounds like the last thing a Mafioso Non Grata might say before his cement Reeboks take him for a stroll along the river bottom. Club. Club. Tiny little word. Means a whole bunch of things. It can mean the tree root a Neanderthal employed to get the attention of a mastodon. It can mean the elegant graphite shafted three-wood that Loren Rubenstein slips out of his golf bag on the seventeenth tee. Club can mean any of thirteen pasteboard rectangles in a common deck of playing cards — or . . . club can refer to something even weirder. It can refer to those strange associations humankind is perversely prone to form.

Clubs. The kind you join up and pay dues to.

There are some bizarre ones out there. Never mind your Shriners and your Kiwanians and your Rotarians and your Girl Guides. How about . . . *The Hollow Earth Society?* Box 63, Houston, Missouri, founded in 1977 to: "launch an expedition by small Zeppelin to the South Polar Aperture and make contact with the people who inhabit the hollow earth."

Too "other-worldly" for you? Then how about *Man Watchers Incorporated.* Women only. Club motto: "It's Our Turn Now."

Or for joiners who've lost their marbles, may I offer the *Marble Collectors Society of America* in Trumball, Connecticut.

Oh yes and there's an *International Tattoo Club* and *Puppeteers of America* and *Turtles International* and even *Uglies Unlimited.*

Something for everybody.

Well, perhaps not everybody. There are people who rise above clubs. Julius Marx, for instance — better known as Groucho. Story goes that Groucho once sent a telegram to the extremely hoity-toity Friars Club, to which he belonged. "Please accept my resignation," the telegram read. "I don't wish to belong to any club that would accept me as a member."

Then there's the story about Victor Mature, who applied for membership at the even more exclusive Los Angeles Country Club. The club secretary sniffed that the club did not accept actors. "I'm no actor," sniffed the veteran ham, "and I've got sixty-four pictures to prove it."

Ah, but my favourite club story involves a turn-of-the-century Englishman by the name of Frederick Edwin Smith, the first Earl of Birkenhead. Lord Birkenhead was by all accounts a stereotypical Upper Crust Tory who said what he liked and did as he pleased and heaven help the mortal who got between the Lord and his goal. So it was that on his way home from the House of Lords each afternoon, Lord Birkenhead would stop in at the incredibly exclusive Athaenium Club. Lord Birkenhead wasn't a member. He just stopped by to . . . use the washroom. But this was the Athaenium Club! Aristocrats and blue-bloods waited decades to be allowed inside its walls. This was an insupportable outrage! Athaenium Club executives bore the blasphemy as long as they could. Finally, one day they dispatched a butler to intercept the Lord on the way back from the washroom. "Excuse me, milord," sniffed the butler, "but are you a member?"

"Good God!" roared Lord Birkenhead, "is this place a club as well?"

I like that. Lord Birkenhead could be in my club anytime.

You Want Boring?
I'll Give You Boring

I've figured out why the Brits won the Battle of Britain.

It's not because they were bigger or stronger or wilier or meaner than their enemy.

It's not because they were better supplied or more highly motivated or because they had God on their side.

It's because the British are incapable of being worn down. They are the George Chuvalo of nations. The Nazis hit them with everything they had, including the kitchen sink. And the Brits just kept . . . being there.

What's the secret of the unflappable, indefatigable British spirit? Boredom threshold. The Brits don't have one. They are incapable of being bored.

Well, look at the training they get. Take the Royal Family. Apart from a few loose shingles like Prince Charles and Princess Margaret, the British Royal family is as tidy and unremarkable a bundle of old sticks as you'll find this side of a thatched roof. They're conventional, predictable, and — not to put too fine a point on it — just a touch boring.

The English are the only people I know who actively encourage their children to join train spotters' clubs. What's a train spotter do? He hangs around train stations copying down the serial number of train engines. When he's cold enough he goes home, pours a cup of tea and rings up other train spotters and they . . . compare engine serial numbers. That's it! That's as exciting as train spotting gets. Only in England, you say? Yes, praise God.

I suppose it ill behooves a Canadian to make mock of British boringness — after all we have curling, Art Eggleton, and London, Ontario.

Ah, but when it comes to serious Ennui Sweepstakes, the Brits have opened a yawning and insurmountable lead. They have the Test Pattern

Club. Actually they call it the Test Card Circle, but it's about test patterns — you know, those static shots you see on television after the programming's finished for the night or before it kicks in in the morning. The most memorable Canadian one I know of showed an Indian chief in the centre with a bunch of numbers all around the perimeter. Well, they have all kinds of test patterns in Britain apparently. Enough to satisfy the eighty-odd members of a British club called The Test Card Circle.

What do the Test Card Circle fanatics actually do to scratch their itch? Well, aside from watching an awful lot of very boring television, they call each other up, swap videos of striking test cards . . . they even have an annual convention where they gather to play a kind of Test Pattern Trivial Pursuit. Sample questions:

"Which types of antennas are most likely to cause ghostings?" and "Who played the music in the middle section of the 1985 BBC tape featuring Markhu Johnston?"

See? If you were a card-carrying member of the Test Circle Club, you'd be able to answer questions like those.

The only question I need to have answered is "why?" Why would a sentient human being, with presumably full use of his faculties, choose to devote a large chunk of his or her leisure time to watching television test patterns? Paul Chatwell, founder of the Test Circle Club says he watches test patterns because the rest of television is a mindless deluge.

Mindless? A quick glance through my TV Guide tells me that today I can catch *America's Funniest Home Videos, Geraldo, Ricki Lake, The Young and the Restless, Roseanne,* and *Pamela Wallin Live.*

Hmmm.

Wonder if the Test Card Circle is looking for international members?

For Old Bags Only

Ever been dumped? I mean well and truly jilted, gulled, left in the lurch, and hung out to dry by the apple of your eye? I guess just about everybody past adolescence has, but commonality does not make it a fun experience.

I remember the first time I got dumped. Sixteen I was. All hormones and strut and Wildroot Cream Oil Charlie. The girl I took it for granted would one day wear my ring and bear my children suddenly got very cool and remote. She insisted — snapped, really — that nothing was wrong, but she looked away and yawned a lot.

Next thing I knew she was dating the quarterback on the senior football team. Oh, the despair, the pain, the humiliation. I was quite certain it was the end of civilization as I knew it.

I can't even remember her name today, but that doesn't mean it didn't hurt. It did, by cracky, it did.

What makes it really tough for Canucks, I think, is that we don't have a Broken Heart Hotline. There's no one you can call; there's no Dumpees Anonymous with a twelve-step recovery program . . . no halfway house you can check into to drink coffee and smoke cigarettes and feel sorry for yourself for a day or two.

What makes it tough on Canucks is that we don't have anything like . . . well, The Old Bags Club of East Garston in England.

A woman by the name of Lady Sarah Graham Moon started the Old Bags Club — right after she discovered that her husband, Sir Peter Graham Moon, was bopping a neighbour woman who lived just down the lane. Well, not *right* after she discovered Sir Peter's little side action. There were several other intermediate steps. First Lady Sarah went through the stages of intense pain. And humiliation. And depression. Then she got P.O.'d — and decided to do something about it.

First she went to the woman's house in the middle of the night, spotted Sir Pete's shiny, red BMW parked in the driveway . . . and poured two gallons of white gloss exterior house paint over it. Then she went back home, got out the pinking shears, and cut the sleeves off thirty-two of his Saville Row suits, custom-made at a thousand quid per . . . Then she raided his prized wine cellar, selected seventy bottles of his best, irreplaceable vintages . . . and went around the East Garston neighbourhood, dropping off a bottle at each doorstep.

Then Lady Sarah formed the Old Bags Club.

It's kind of a support group for abandoned wives — although that description makes it sound forlorn and poor-me-ish. The Old Bags Club isn't like that at all. It's fun and feisty. The only condition for membership is that the applicant be a recent dumpee . . . and that she have at least the tattered remnants of a sense of humour.

Women who need the Old Bags Club tend to find out about it. "Last Sunday," says Lady Sarah, "this shaking wreck of a woman arrived with her hair falling down her face, and we spent the afternoon together with some friends and she left calm and comforted. She was not mended, of course, but she had found some chums and had some fun."

Some chums, some fun — that's about as good as the Immediate After Dump Period gets . . . until the healing poultice of time gets to work its slow magic. I would have settled for some chums and some fun back when old What's Her Name dumped me.

I would have been happy if somebody had just explained to me that hearts don't really break. It just feels that way for a while.

I would have been happy if old What's Her Name had been Lynda Barry the comedian. Lynda's the one who said: "Love is the exploding cigar we all willingly smoke."

So. Ya gotta light?

Japan: You've Come a Long Way, Unfortunately

Take a look at the Japanese. They have virtually no resources. All they have going for them are 90 million over-achievers! Think what the Japanese would give for Canada's resources!

PRESIDENT, DOW CHEMICAL COMPANY

Yep, pretty impressive, the story of Japan. "One huge processing plant," someone called the country, "scouring the world for raw materials."

It's an amazing story when you think about it. Just a generation ago, Japan was prostrate. Slapped flat by the Allied Forces. Defenceless. Yenless. Forced to accept handouts from the rest of the world.

And today? The *Economist* magazine recently did a study of Japanese real estate. Overall value: 17 *trillion* Canadian dollars. In case you're wondering what that looks like, it's:

$17,000,000,000,000.00.

Or, as the *Economist* explained it: "In theory, Japan can buy the whole of America by selling off Metropolitan Tokyo, or all of Canada by hawking the grounds of the Imperial Palace."

How did the Japanese manage to accomplish all that in less than half a century? In a word — sweat. A Japanese schoolteacher would collapse in disbelief if he saw the soft ride Canadian schoolkids get. And it doesn't stop with the graduation ceremony. Your typical Japanese working stiff — white collar, blue collar, and no collar at all — gives a helluva lot more than you or I would ever dream of putting out. An average Japanese office worker puts in about 2,250 hours at his or her desk every year. That's about six *weeks* more than the average North American office worker. As a spokesman named Yukio

163

Matsuyama explained: "The Japanese are addicted to tension as a welcome way of life, as a stimulating springboard for individual and collective advancement."

Mind you, there is a price tag for all that workaholism. It's called *karoshi* — literally, "death by overworking." It's the second biggest killer in the country according to a recent Japanese Ministry of Health report.

There are other signs that all is not rosy in the Land of the Rising Sun. A new business has opened in Tokyo in which actors and actresses visit lonely old people and "pretend" to be their sons and daughters. The actors feign contrition and shame, while the old folks "scold" them for not visiting more often. Price tag for this little fantasy play: $1,100 per therapy session.

And there are indications that the next generation of Japanese might not be quite so dedicated. The Japanese who hauled themselves out of the rubble of World War II have — as parents have everywhere — made certain that their children don't endure the same hardships. That's why, according to a recent study, more than half of Japanese children own televisions, radios, and tape recorders. A third of them have their own telephones as well.

And they're fat. Japanese kids scorn the traditional rice-based diet of their parents. They want junk food. The kind they see on TV. Researchers asked them what their favourite activity was. Most frequent answer: watching television.

Japanese child psychologists say it's even worse when the kids hit their teens. "They have no interest in anything," says one expert. "They live from day to day with no goal in life."

Hmmm. Now where have I heard that before?

To paraphrase a cigarette ad, you've come a long way, *tomo dachi.*

I've Been Hijacked

I don't like to whine and I hate to cause a scene, but, uh . . . I've just been hijacked?

It happened at an airport — where most hijackings happen. The Vancouver International Airport in this case. I had just jettisoned my luggage, been spread-eagled by a baton-wielding Rent a Cop at security, and was making my way to Gate 18B for a flight to Toronto when I rounded a corner and ran smack into . . .

Checkpoint Charlie.

It wasn't called that, but it might as well have been. It was a wall, manned by tight-lipped security personnel. All it needed was a couple of rows of razor wire and a searchlight or two strobing across the terrazzo No Man's Land that separated my moccasins from their Doc Watsons.

"What's this all about?" I asked in my best, long-suffering Canuck voice. "A pre-boarding fee," the smiling mannequin before me explained. If I still wanted to catch flight 843 to Toronto, it was going to cost me an extra $10.

"For what?" I mewed.

"Airport Improvement," the mannequin purred.

Well now, here's an inspirational Canadian scam worthy of the Boyd Gang or the Silver Fox himself. You've got a captive audience made up of poor schlemiels already separated from their luggage and nervously in transit to someplace else. You stop them halfway to the plane and tell them it's going to cost them more than they thought.

Wasn't that the M.O. of Jesse James and Robin Hood?

What are the targets going to do — lie down on the terrazzo? Threaten to stage a sit-in? (And live on airport food? Get serious.)

Besides, it's only a little extortion. You're not asking them for their life savings. Just ten bucks a head if they're heading out of province. Fifteen bucks for international travellers. Hey. That's less than the mob charges to watch over your pizza joint.

I paid my ten bucks under protest. (Hey, it's Canada so they even had a printed form available for people who wanted to complain.) I paid, but it left a bad taste in my mouth. As I strapped myself in for flight 843 Boeing 737 nonstop service to Toronto, I found myself wishing I'd been stroppier and said, "No, I'm not paying your damned Airport User Fee. I already bought and paid for my ticket and my luggage is aboard and what are you gonna do about it?"

But I didn't. And I don't suppose most other people who fly through Vancouver International Airport raise much of a fuss about the Airport Improvement Fee, either. Which means other airports are going to look at it and stroke their corporate chins and say, "Hmmm . . . worked in Vancouver. Why don't we give it a try?"

And you know just between you and me, I wouldn't mind so much if the airline service was a little more helpful.

I mean last month I went up to the check-in desk and said, "I'm checking two bags here. I'd like you to send this garment bag to Inuvik and this packsack to Fredericton."

"I'm sorry, sir," sniffed the ticket agent. "We can't possibly do that."

"Why not?" I asked. "You did it last month."

6

The World Around Us

Trees I Have Loved

I think that I shall never see
A poem lovely as a tree.

JOYCE KILMER

It would be tempting to blame Joyce Kilmer for the outbreak of
unabashed Tree Love that's going around these days. Tempting, but
not fair. Mister Kilmer penned his immortal lines in the early years
of this century, whereas humankind has been making Goo Goo eyes
at trees for millennia — probably since the day we shinnied down
them and started living on the ground.

The Druids worshipped trees. Mayans and Visigoths and Polynesians
and Laps and Maoris all bowed down, in one way or another, to trees.
Small wonder that here in the twentieth century, arboreal activists from
Vancouver and North York, Seattle and Scarborough, eagerly scramble
to get arrested in defence of the Ancient Growth Forests around Lake
Temagami and Clayquot Sound.

Our love affair with our leafy brethren is one that's been percolating
for some time.

Tree hugging is as natural a human activity as line dancing, cursing
the post office, and making love.

And nowhere more than in England. I just read an item about a
group called Tree Spirit, which has its headquarters in Worcester,
England. Members of Tree Spirit don't merely hug trees, they chat with
them, pass along tree gossip, even lay their heads on the tree roots for
personal psychotherapy.

"Whenever we travel," says an editorial in *Tree Spirit* magazine, "we
talk to the trees where we camp. We tell them of the beautiful trees
where we live . . . we tell them about the weather in places other than
their own."

Further on, the editorial advises readers to share their deepest feelings and secrets, treating the trees like a close friend.

"You can trust a tree," confides the magazine. "It will never tell anyone else."

No, I suppose not.

Martin Blount is editor of the *Tree Spirit* magazine and founder of the organization. It began a little more than ten years ago with a small campaign to save a grove of oak trees threatened by a proposed subdivision. Martin and his band of merry tree huggers saved the oaks and just . . . branched out from there.

Today, there are over a hundred members across England. They don't just protest and march and write letters. Most of their energy goes into planting saplings of native species.

Martin Blount is very much attached to trees. He believes that different species have specific personalities. "Silver birches are very feminine and happy and joyous. But they don't live very long — seventy or eighty years. Nothing for a tree. Yews can live for a thousand years. They grow so slowly. They've seen a lot of things. They are very wise trees."

An infidel is tempted to ask, if they're so wise, how come so many trees wind up as firewood, telephone poles, and Kleenex? Martin Blount has an answer for that. He doesn't see the act of chopping down trees as ethically indefensible.

"You have to go out and explain the situation to the tree. You have to tell the tree why you're doing it. You show the tree respect and then you thank it for its timber."

And when you think about it, wal-nut? It's chestnut fair. Oh, elm not saying we should pine or make ashes of ourselves, but maple we'd be more poplar if we didn't go around aspen fir trouble. I think that's why we get sycamore than we yewsed to. If we could just cedar way clear to spruce up a little and not lilac we do, things would be A-oak-A. Butternut to wait until we've cottonwood splinters in our backsides — willow join with me and turn over a new leaf now?

Life doesn't have to be a beech, you know.

Cultivate Your Garden

Potatoes are pretty much a latecomer. When Spanish explorers first showed up in Europe with boatloads of the gnarly South American tubers, Europeans recoiled. They thought potatoes were demon spawn. And that was in the 1500s, a mere four and a bit centuries ago. Now your beans . . . they go back much further. Eight thousand years, at least. And wheat? That's the granddaddy of them all. Stone Age tribes around the Mediterranean were growing, harvesting, and baking wheat into bread ten thousand years ago.

What are we talking about here? Gardens. The joy of. A nineteenth-century writer by the name of Charles Dudley Warner said it as well as any green-thumbed, aching backed, two-legged dirt disturber ever did. "To own a bit of ground," wrote Warner, "To scratch it with a hoe, to plant seeds, and watch the renewal of life — this is the commonest delight of the race, the most satisfactory thing a man can do."

He's right, you know. It's a singularly satisfying thing, to cultivate a garden. A vegetable garden, I'm talking about. I know some folks like to raise dahlias and cacti and exotic orchid varieties. But I come from peasant stock and I like to eat what I grow.

I also like the moral simplicity of the vegetable garden. There is very little grey out there among the tomato plants and the cucumber mounds. No amending formulas. No notwithstanding clauses. If you tend your garden faithfully, chances are pretty good you will be rewarded. If you do a half-assed job the way you brush your teeth and sing "O Canada" and do your Christmas shopping, then before you know it, your garden will look like a close-up of Johnny Rotten's hairline and you'll be buying your veggies in blister packs.

Story goes that Samuel Coleridge got into a wrangle with a man who believed that children should be raised as free spirits, unencumbered by formal instruction. That way, said Coleridge's guest, the child would be free to make his own decisions when he matured. Coleridge nodded and rubbed his chin and, after a decent interval, asked the man if he'd like to take a turn around the garden. Coleridge opened his back door onto . . . what wasn't much more than a vacant lot. "You call this a garden," snorted the visitor. "There are nothing but weeds here."

"Not at all," replied Coleridge. "I simply didn't wish to infringe upon the liberty of the garden in any way. I was just giving the garden a chance to express itself and to choose its own production."

Exactly. You've heard the expression, "No atheists in foxholes?" Well, you'll find damn few liberals around the garden centres, either.

Not that gardening's a cakewalk. Lots of problems. From microscopic kamikaze creepy crawlys to ravenous deer that can jump a six-foot fence. From late frosts to early snow; from arid rows of parched plants to soggy plots that look like Vietnamese rice paddies. Gardening is never perfect. But provided you're not trying to work a hundred acres or grow dirigible-sized zucchinis, gardening's pretty simple. Good soil, water, sunshine — and stay on top of the weeds.

Plus, the garden offers sensual delights long before harvest time. There's the pleasurable sight of sturdy plants doing well. The murmur of bees and other sundry buzzers ferrying nectar and pollen from your garden to . . . well, theirs, I guess. AND the feel of freshly hoed garden loam oozing like granulated velvet between your toes on a hot summer afternoon. That's the most fun you can have with your overalls on.

There's an old Chinese saying that goes: "If you wish to be happy for an hour, get drunk. If you wish to be happy for three days, get married. If you wish to be happy for a week, kill your pig and eat it. If you wish to be happy forever, cultivate a garden."

Well, I don't know about forever happy — but you'll have your hands full. Not to mention the spaces between your toes.

O Tannenbaum

You like trees? I like trees. The writer Willa Cather liked trees. Willa Cather wrote: "I like trees because they seem more resigned to the way they have to live than other things do." Yeah, resigned. I guess that's a good word to describe all the old trees I see by the road every January. Another good word would be "abandoned."

Christmas trees, I mean. Never felt entirely comfortable about the whole concept of the Christmas tree. Oh, I love to look at 'em and decorate 'em — and, I confess, I love to go out in the wood with my trusty hatchet and chop them down once a year. But I've always felt vaguely guilty about it. The way I feel when I'm riding in a big American land yacht like an Oldsmobile or a Lincoln. I know it's a gas guzzler, I know I'm polluting, but God it's nice to ride without your knees up around your ears for a change.

Well, then — the Christmas tree. Stands to reason that there's something aberrational about millions of families rushing out to grab an evergreen for their living rooms once a year, doesn't it?

Maybe it doesn't. During the holidays I met a farmer at a party, and over a glass or two of eggnog, I confessed my tannenbaum angst. He shook his head and smiled, like he'd heard it before.

Then he told me about his farm. Not a farm, really — two hundred acres of rocks and wild grass when he took it over fifteen years ago. Too marginal for wheat and too hilly and stony to plough. Farmers had given up on it decades ago.

This guy planted Scotch pine and spruce seedlings back in the late seventies. A couple of years ago, he took off his first crop of Christmas trees . . . six, eight feet tall. And all these years he's had the pleasure of watching chickadees and chipmunks, squirrels, porcupine, deer, grosbeaks, cardinals, bluebirds, indigo buntings, sparrows, all living on and in the trees he grew. He still has that pleasure because he only harvests a few acres a year, as the trees grow to maturity. And he keeps replanting, so the cycle goes on. As he told me, "I put trees where there were no trees before and I keep replacing them. They produce food and shelter for animals and oxygen for all of us — so what's the problem?"

Well, the problem is knee-jerk environmentalism. The idea that all tree cutting is evil and cutting Christmas trees is the same as chainsawing the rain forest. It's not. It's more like reaping barley or soybeans. As the farmer told me, "Christmas trees are a seasonal crop — like daffodils in the spring or pumpkins in the fall. They just take a little longer, that's all."

Makes me feel better about the whole idea of Christmas trees, that farmer. Makes me feel better about all the sad, old, browning Christmas trees you see lying on their sides wearing wisps of tinsel at the curb, waiting for garbage disposal. A lot of municipalities pick up the trees and chip them into compost these days . . . but even if they go right to the dump, trees will break down a lot faster than your average Reddi Whip Aerosol can or used Pampers.

Besides, what's the alternative to a real, bristling, aromatic Christmas tree? A plastic tree? No thanks. I've got two Yuletide words for plastic trees and those words are Bah and Humbug.

The Bad News: It's a Monster. The Good News: It's Vegetarian

Do you remember corny old Monster Movies? *Mothra. King Kong. The Creature from the Black Lagoon.* Not to mention those Japanese bargain basement brutes like *Rodan* — and my personal favourite, *Godzilla.*

For those of you who chose not to rot your cerebellums on this junk, Godzilla was a four-hundred-foot-high Lizard critter untimely nudged from the mists of prehistory. For millions of years he had slumbered peacefully under the earth's mantle somewhere off the coast of Japan until disturbed by meddling human nuclear scientists. Godzilla woke up very cranky. He took out his bad mood and his blowtorch breath on a people-stomping rampage over hill and dale of old Nippon, flattening villages, incinerating condos, and playing crack the whip with commuter trains until . . .

But I won't ruin it for you. Godzilla will be on the Late Show one of these nights.

You really ought to watch these old celluloid creakers if you can. You'd be amazed at some of the unexpectedly familiar faces you can pick out if you look closely. Would you believe Perry Mason in *Godzilla*? Yep, the actor Raymond Burr is there — although it's easy to see why he missed an Oscar nomination that year.

And check out the movie *Them* next time you get a chance. Sharp-eyed viewers will be able to winkle out Davy Crockett (Fess Parker), Marshall Matt Dillon (James Arness), and the unmistakeably angular features of an unsmiling Leonard Nimoy.

I guess Mister Spock must have taken an extra acting job while he waited for his executive appointment to the Starship Enterprise to come through.

I've always been fond of the fictional monster heroes, but I never thought I'd see the day when there would be a real one to get goosebumps over.

I was wrong.

How about this for a monster profile: a creature that dwells underground, is at least fifteen centuries old, feeds on dead and decaying matter, weighs at least ten tons, is impervious to fire, and . . .

. . . is bigger than twenty-five Maple Leaf Gardens put together.

Oh yes, and one more thing.

It's alive. Here. Right now.

And I'm not kidding.

Armillaria Bulbosa can be found in a huge hardwood forest tucked away in the northwest corner of Michigan, near the Wisconsin border. Scientists have confirmed that it's there; that it has survived at least one giant forest fire; and that it has been living quietly in that hardwood forest since about 1,000 years before Columbus took his famous westward cruise from Spain.

A couple of other attributes that should put *Armillaria Bulbosa* in the Horror Hall of Fame: it is impossible to decapitate. If you lop off one section of it, it doesn't even wince. In fact, if you got a giant machete and chopped *Armillaria Bulbosa* in half, do you know what you'd get?

Two *Armillaria Bulbosas*.

Just so you can sleep tonight, I should tell you that the creature under discussion here is a fungus. The largest fungus ever discovered, but a fungus for all that.

If you went to the hardwood forest where *Armillaria Bulbosa* lives and stuck a spade in the forest floor, you would hit the fungus with your first shovelful. But all you would see would be white fibrous threads running every which direction.

That's it. Aside from some sweet-smelling mushrooms that appear above ground once in a while, that's all there is to *Armillaria Bulbosa*. Except that there's a helluva lot of those threads underground — about forty acres' worth.

And anything that big has got to have some potential in the

Hollywood Horror movie market. What it needs is a sexier name. *The Monster Mushroom That Masticated Michigan*, maybe. Or how about, *The Humongous Fungus?*

Whatever they call the movie, I'll buy a ticket.

And the next time I bend down to pick a mushroom, I'm going to ask permission first.

Dinosaur Droppings

I've got a stone sitting on top of my computer monitor. It's a hard lump of muddy brown rock about the size of two hockey pucks melted together. I use it to hold down papers and to heft in my hand whenever I'm stuck for words. It's not pretty, and it's not worth anything by jewellers' standards — but it's not just a rock, either. My rock is a coprolite. That's a twenty-five-cent word that means fossilized dinosaur poop, to put it bluntly.

I keep my coprolite on my computer monitor because it helps me to keep things in perspective, and to remind me what a bunch of Johnny-come-latelies we big-brained, soft-pawed, hairless bipeds are on this strutting stage called Earth. The dinosaurs were here long before we were — 65 million years ago as near as scientists can figure. Human beings are kind of like Crayola — we come in a variety of colours but pretty much the same shape and size. Dinosaurs came anywhere from chicken-little to behemoths bigger than three city buses bumper to bumper. Temperamentally they ran the gamut from gentle watercress munchers to horrific, flesh-rending marauders that would have used Arnold the Terminator for an hors d'oeuvre.

Dinosaurs were the Lords of the Universe in a way that Conrad Black could only have wet dreams about.

And yet . . . they disappeared. Vanished. They were snuffed out in a geological flash. For a hundred million years they ruled the Earth as Stalin ruled Russia. And then they were gone. How? Why? What can their passing teach us?

It can teach us not to be too cocky. The latest theory on dinosaur disappearance has it that things were going swimmingly for the reptiles until one afternoon about 65 million years ago, when the creatures looked up from their munching and rending and coprolite producing to behold a black spot in the sky. It was an asteroid heading straight for Earth at an estimated speed of twenty-five miles per second.

The asteroid, which weighed 500 billion tons, smashed into the earth's crust not far off the Yucatán Peninsula in Mexico. It wasn't huge, as asteroids go — only about five miles across — but its impact caused a quantum hiccup in the development of life on earth. There were colossal tidal waves that smashed into grazing brontosaurs and quizzical triceratops, shredding them like so many papier-mâché floats. There were horizon-to-horizon dust storms obliterating the sky, choking the breath out of tyrannosaurs and pterodactyls alike. There was instant winter — temperature drops so severe and instantaneous that the forests would have been flash-frozen.

And fires, of course. Jungle and forest fires everywhere. For any large beasts that were not pulverized, or asphyxiated, or fried, or frozen at impact, the future would be painful and short-lived. Nitric acid from the sky would serve to leach cadmium, lead, and mercury out of the rocks and into the water systems, rendering them poisonous.

The thing that comes home to me as I hold my coprolite is that this all happened in a matter of hours. Dinosaurs would have safely grazed and had dominion over all they surveyed for a hundred million years . . . only to see it all end in a couple of days at most. Paleontologists have called it "the worst weekend in the history of the world."

I think about that weekend a lot as I stare at my blank computer screen, fretting about deadlines, the mortgage, speeding tickets, and Jean Chrétien's latest bon mot.

And I fondle my coprolite some more.

Certainly puts Canada's constitutional crisis in perspective.

The Sound of One Dog Barking

This is a column about my dog. Rufus is a podgy, middle-aged mutt who came into my life under false pretences. The pet store owner assured me, as he was pocketing my cheque for ninety bucks, that the bundle of fur in the cardboard box was pure Australian shepherd.

I didn't know what an Australian shepherd was, but it sounded kind of exotic, so I bought him.

That was eleven years ago. Now, I know what an Australian shepherd looks like.

And my dog isn't one.

Mind you, he'd be the Arnold Schwarzenegger of Australian shepherds if he was one. Australian shepherds are mid-size dogs, built light and wiry for all that shepherding they have to do. My dog tips the scales at eighty-five pounds. He carries his bulk under a coat of short black hair tastefully touched up at the legs and tail tip with splashes of white.

Fitting that he should sport the colours of a Holstein, since he's almost as wide as one.

He certainly doesn't have the metabolism of a working farm dog. If Rufus moved any less, he'd have to be reclassified as a garden plant. Rufus's idea of a perfect day is one spent lying on his back with his tongue lolling out the side of his mouth while he passes gas. He doesn't sit up, beg, fetch sticks, or roll over on command. He's scared of cats, not fussy about other dogs, and basically a bit of a chicken-bleep when it comes to anything that moves.

But he does have one unsurpassed talent, my Rufus.

He can bark.

Lord, can he bark.

To knock on the front door of my house is to unleash a firestorm of barks and woofs that shiver the timbers and rattle the windows and cause roof shingles to curl.

It's a weird thing, dogs barking. A kind of neurotic habit they picked up when they became domesticated. Wolves only bark when they're young. As they mature, wolves develop a more sophisticated language of guttural growls and snarls. But not dogs.

"They're immature, like teenagers," says biologist Raymond Coppinger, "very hard to train."

That certainly fits Rufus. I've tried everything from dog biscuits to verbal threats and banishment to the basement. Rufus just keeps on barking.

Apparently, I'm lucky. Rufus ONLY barks when somebody comes to the door. Doctor Coppinger claims that dogs may bark at the moon, at the wind, or just for the hell of it. He once clocked a sheep dog in Minnesota that barked nonstop for seven hours.

At, as far as Doctor Coppinger could tell, nothing in particular.

Back in the old days when we hung out in caves and carried clubs and spears, it must have been dandy to have four-legged burglar alarms sleeping beside you. Dogs smell and hear intruders long before dozy old Homo sapiens do.

Which, I guess, is all Rufus is doing when he barks. He's telling the rest of us — members of his "pack" — that there's a sabre-toothed tiger on the front porch.

Did you know that dogs bark in different languages? According to a report called "A Glossary of Sounds Made by Dogs and Cats," pooches say "bow-wow" here in Canada, and "haf-haf" in Czechoslovakia. In Greece they go "rav-rav"; in Spain, "guau-guau." Taiwanese dogs say "wang-wang"; Laotian dogs,"voon-voon."

I think I'll read this report to Rufus.

If he's going to bark, he might as well learn a few languages.

Batman Exposed!

Ever wakened from a dead sleep to a saucer-eyed awareness that you were not alone in your bedroom? We did. Last Thursday. Yours truly and my Helpmeet Against Life's Trials, Lynne. Spooky. We didn't hear drawers sliding open or jewellery chinking, or stealthy footsteps padding across the floor. It was more like something just over the threshold of sound . . . like balled-up Kleenexes being lobbed around the room. Then we heard a whispering *thppp thppp*. At the bottom of the bed? Over by the dresser?

But the sound was gone, almost before it registered. We stared into the black but saw nothing — or wait! No, must have been blinking. But there it is again! Just a whiplash across the retina, faster than a politician's smile.

Then I knew. It wasn't a burglar we had in our bedroom. It was a bat.

There's a critter that sure got short-changed in English. Bat. What a pathetically inadequate name. The Aztecs called them butterfly mice. In French they're *chauve souris* — bald mice. The Germans have the best name of all: *Fledermaus*. That's the one we Anglos could have stolen! We could have called them Flittermice. But no . . . we stuck them with the mundane, monosyllabic "bat."

My bedroom intruder was just a little brown bat, but cute as he was and Harrowsmithy as I like to think I am, it's tough to doze off knowing that something that looks like a miniature crime crusader is barrel-rolling through airspace not all that far from your pillow.

Which is why I got up, nude, at 2:30 Thursday morning and put on my duck boots. So I could go out in the backyard shed and rummage through my fishing stuff, till I found my old landing net. And okay,

I admit it, while I was out there I picked up my bicycle helmet, too, because, well, bats are skittish and they have teeth and claws and I wouldn't want him to mistake my head for a runway or anything.

It's not easy to catch a bat in even a good-sized landing net, but I did it. Well, truth to tell he flew into the net while I was adjusting my chin strap. Point is, I got the bat in the landing net and took him out in the backyard at 2:37 a.m., in the nude, in my duck boots. And I was just kind of holding the netted bat out in front of me and trying to remove the mesh from his wings with a hockey stick, because I didn't want to get too close to a ticked-off bat — even with my bicycle helmet on. And I just about had him free when . . . I hear the car door slam.

My next-door neighbours coming home from a party. So close I could hear their house keys rattling. No sweat, I said to myself. I'll just stand perfectly still. It's dark. They won't see me.

Nor would they have, if my boon companion and pillar of strength against Life's buffeting, Lynne, hadn't chosen that moment to throw on the backyard floodlights. "Need some light dear?" I heard her call cheerily.

NO, not really. A black hole would be nice. Or perhaps a cyanide lozenge . . .

The bat flew off. I wished that I could. And my neighbours? You know, I don't know what my neighbours made of it. Haven't seen or heard a peep out of them since Thursday morning.

Not surprised really. Last time I saw them they were looking at me like I had . . .

flittermice in my belfry.

Of All the Saints, I Like Bernard Best

So far in this life, I've only had to take babies from their mother once. It was for their own good, but, of course, the mother couldn't see that. She was, frankly, a bitch. But that's only fitting, because the babies involved were puppies. Saint Bernards, as a matter of fact. Heidi was the mother, and she'd go about 210 pounds even when she wasn't pregnant. She had decided to have her litter under an abandoned dock down by the river. This was not a good idea because the water level of the river was unpredictable. One heavy rain and those pups would be gone. As a small and supple adolescent, it was my job to crawl under the dock, reason briefly with the mother, and get those puppies out of there.

Ever looked a Saint Bernard in the eye, close-up? A mother, I mean, whose newborn little ones you were about to take away from her? They're big . . . Saint Bernards. They've got teeth you could hang your parka on and a jaw the size of a forklift. Seems that way when you're splayed out on your belly under a dock, nose to nose.

I cooed and I cajoled and I eventually gingerly picked those six pups up two by two and carried them out. And those massive, brown, mother Saint Bernard eyes watched my every move like a lioness watching a nervy field mouse and she never so much as rumbled a growl at me.

I wouldn't try that with a fox terrier. Heck, I'd wear heavy gloves before I tried it with a parakeet . . . but Saint Bernards? They're different. They're special. Strong as an ox but gentle as a lamb. That's why the Augustinian monks bred the dogs in the first place. The monks lived in a hospice at a pass high in the Swiss Alps, where blizzards were sudden and treacherous, obliterating every landmark as far as the squinted eye could see. But the Saint Bernards, on their pie-plate paws, were steadfast and reliable and unfailingly gentle, and their thick coats made them impervious to the weather.

Saint Bernards have been playing mountain lifeguards in the Alps since the time of Peter the Great. One of them, a gentle giant named Barry, saved forty snowbound souls in his career. The monks say that, altogether, more than 2,500 people have been rescued by the gallant dogs.

But perhaps not for much longer. Some folks don't like the Saint Bernard as a rescue dog. They're too big, they say. Not mobile enough. Not agile. Not adaptable to other climates. Like the stately Studebaker and the overloaded Oldsmobile, the Saint Bernard model is being retired, in favour of sleeker, more stripped-down models. Shepherds, retrievers, and the like. All fine dogs, to be sure. But not quite as noble as the Saint Bernard.

The humorist Josh Billings once defined a dog as the only thing on Earth that loves you more than he loves himself. I think the Saint Bernard exemplifies that. And I know if I ever got lost in a blizzard or stranded in an avalanche, lost to the point of numbness, weariness, disorientation, and despair, the sight of a set of slobbery jowls flanking a big, wet, black nose, surmounted by a pair of huge, moist, infinitely sad brown eyes would be just about the most glorious sight I could hope to see. Along with the brandy keg, of course.

Mind you, at that point I'd probably settle for a Chihuahua with a thermos of cocoa around its neck.

Don't Mess with Elephants

I'll never forget something my father told me when I was just a little kid. We were at the circus watching some Jumbo or Dumbo plodding around the ring doing stupid tricks in a dopey hat. My father leaned over and whispered: "An elephant . . . never forgets." *Never?* I thought. Never forgets *anything*? No wonder they had such big heads.

I never forgot that.

Turns out the old wives' tale isn't far off the mark. Animal trainers will tell you that, while elephants aren't necessarily Einsteins when it comes to learning new behaviour, once an idea is locked in that mighty cranium, it's probably there for life.

Elephant . . . ele-phant . . . the name is at least as strange as the creature that wears it. It comes from an ancient Greek word *elephas*, meaning — guess what? — ivory. Figures. Man looks at one of the most fantastical creatures on the planet, big as a house, ears like bed-sheets, legs like dock pilings, a fire hose for a schnozz — and what does man see? He sees those shiny money-making toothpicks hanging down in front.

The elephant has paid dearly for those tusks. They only have one natural, earthly enemy and as Pogo might say, he is us. We've killed a lot of elephants. Over the centuries, elephants have been snared, leg trapped, and driven over cliffs and into pits, not to mention poisoned and shot with everything from spears to high-powered rifles to bazookas. But unlike the buffalo, the dodo, the passenger pigeon, the cod — elephants do not always go gently. There's a tremendous familial instinct among them. A train crew in rural India found that out a while back when their locomotive knocked down and killed an elephant calf. No sooner had they got the train stopped than they heard what sounded like eleven or twelve more freight trains approaching. Through the forest. Fast. It was the rest of the herd responding to the calf's distress cries. The elephant herd surrounded the corpse on the tracks and then they sat down, refusing to move. The crew spent a few fruitless hours trying to budge them, then gave up, put the train in reverse, and took it back to the station.

That crew got off lightly. A few years ago a herd of seventeen Indian elephants stampeded and killed thirty-three people when timber cutters encroached on their food supply. In Sri Lanka, elephants responded to attacks by Tamil guerrillas with a guerrilla charge of their own, which left nine people dead.

And when elephants get mad, it's not just the bulls. The retaliation can be co-ed or even Amazonian. In the southern Sudan, there's a band of elephants that went down in the record books as the Suffragette Herd. All girls. Their stomping ground was a 250-mile chunk of the southern Sudan. They ran it tighter than Capone ran Chicago.

Not that elephants are winning or anything. Elephants don't have guns or aphrodisiac fantasies. Most of all, they lack that quintessential human gene that makes it okay to slaughter a fellow Earth tenant for his eyeteeth.

And slaughter them we have. In one decade — the 1980s — ivory poachers reduced the African elephant population from 1.3 million to a little over six hundred thousand. Cut the continental population in half in ten years.

Are elephants doomed? Perhaps not. There are signs that we're finally smartening up. Most African countries have passed laws and beefed up poacher patrols to save their elephant stocks. And I would think that the "let's-bag-an-elephant" safaris must be dead. A man or a woman would have to be a singular dork to want to play Great White Hunter in the 1990s.

Let's hope we're smartening up. Because elephants are beautiful. And because they're peaceful when left alone. And because they're big.

And most of all because . . . they never forget.

This Is Hunting?

The average full-grown red fox (*Vulpes vulpes*) weighs less than fifteen pounds and measures a little over four feet from wet black nose to the tip of his long fluffy tail.

Terror-wise, the red fox is distinctly bad news for rabbits, squirrels, partridges, mice, and moles — plus the odd domestic chicken if he can find one. But the fox is no threat to any human and he's certainly no match for a dog. Any dog. Even a Pekinese or a Pomeranian.

Which makes you wonder why the British feel it's necessary, every year, to unleash twenty thousand specially trained hunting dogs and fifty thousand mounted horsemen with no other purpose than to scare up foxes, hunt them down, and rip them to shreds.

The fox hunt: "the unspeakable in pursuit of the uneatable," Oscar Wilde called it. There are more than thirty packs of hunting dogs in England. They take part in about two hundred "hunts," which run down and tear apart eight to thirteen thousand foxes each year.

Not all Britons approve, naturally. In fact, 80 percent of them would like to relegate the sport to the same oblivion occupied by bull-baiting, cock-fighting, and witch-burning. A few years back, a bill to abolish fox hunting was only narrowly defeated in the British Parliament.

When you think about it, what kind of a Cro-Magnon could possibly argue *in favour* of such a barbaric pastime? Who would actually choose to spend their weekends (and several thousand quid) on the back of some huge horse while dressed in drag, crashing through trees and over fences, trying to run a fifteen-pound animal to death?

Well, someone like Maxwell Rumney, certainly. He is a master of the Trinity Foot Beagles, a group of hunt fanciers who have galumphed over the hills and dales of Cambridgeshire since 1862.

"We simply are out here to watch the hounds work, for the thrill of the chase," explains Rumney.

Codswallop. Unhappily for fox hunters, technology has caught up with them. Last fall, an anti-hunting activist with a concealed video camera managed to infiltrate the Quorn — the most blue-blooded of England's hunts. As a result, we now know what really happens when the fox, exhausted, "goes to earth."

What happens — as the video camera showed — is that two-legged hunters dig the terrified animal out of its den, grab it by the scruff of its neck, and throw it, alive, to the slavering hounds, which rip it to pieces.

"Only the huntsmen used to see what went on," said a spokesman. This time, all of Britain saw it as the film was run on national television. Within a week, more than two thousand indignant citizens had joined the swelling ranks of the League Against Cruel Sports.

LACS is just one group that's sprung up to try to bury the fox hunt once and for all. There's also a crew called the Hunt Saboteurs Association. They crash the hunts while they're in progess, laying false scents to throw off the hounds, and blowing fake "Tally Ho's" to confuse the hunters.

Naturally the "squirearchy" is incensed. They see themselves as beset upon by Philistines and Bolsheviks.

"They feel that we should get rid of tradition at the drop of a hat," harrumphs Maxwell Rumney.

Which reminds me of the great riposte by Winston Churchill. When he was secretary of the Navy, Churchill made a proposal that offended one of his Admiral advisors.

"But sir," the Admiral replied, "your proposal goes against naval tradition."

"Naval tradition?" growled Churchill. "What is naval tradition? Rum, sodomy, and the lash!"

Maybe the Brits could swing a deal here. The fox hunters give up terrorizing small defenceless animals. In return, British Parliament enshrines the right of Mister Rumney and friends to indulge in unlimited booze, buggery, and beating each other with whips.

The Dissing of
Summer Lawns

Friends . . . Canucks . . . Countrymen . . . Lend me your ears. I come to speak not of law and order . . . but of lawn disorder. My lawn, your lawn. That patch of crabgrass, dandelion, and unsolicited doggy doo at the front of the house. Take a look at it.

Is there anything sadder than the sight of a Canadian lawn in early spring — all yellow and littered with a winter's detritus?

Well, yes, there is at least one thing sadder than the pathetic sight of *my* front lawn. What's sadder is what I am about to do to that lawn. I plan to rake it. I plan to roll it. I plan to take a nasty-looking spiked drum and aerate it. And following those operations, I will systematically and methodically strafe that lawn with phosphates, nitrates, sulphates — whatever drugs it takes to transform my lacklustre patch of thatch into a pulsating, verdant, Ben Johnsonian state of exaggerated health.

If things go the way I plan and the folks back at Mastercard control don't yank my plastic, I expect by June to have a lawn that would put the Honduran Rainforest to shame; a lawn positively athrob with aggressive, thrusting, serried, row-on-row of grass blades. And then . . . and then . . .

And then I will spend the rest of my summer right up until first frost, sweating like a navvy behind my Toro as I try to hold the lawn back.

Because surprise, surprise, the lawn grows faster than Rush Limbaugh's worst nightmare about LSD in the drinking fountain. It thrives. It flourishes. And I spend my entire summer like the guerrilla leader of some resistance movement, trying to stop the inexorable advance of the Nazoid Green Monster just beyond the front steps.

Lawns just don't make any sense. Well, the combination of home owners and lawns doesn't make any sense.

Take the situation in Stratford, Ontario. Stratford City Council, after much deliberation, has decided to grant Stratford citizen John Sardo permission to keep three goats. Mister Sardo lives on a fenced-off property in Stratford and the reason he wants to keep goats is that his property is too hilly and rocky to cut with a lawnmower. No problem for the goats, of course. They can scramble anywhere and keep the grass clipped becomingly short.

My question is: Haven't we got things backwards? How come somebody has to get permission to keep goats? Think about it. Goats are quiet, not hard to look at — fascinating, really — and as they eat the grass that drives homeowners nuts, they also fertilize the ground they chomp.

But a lawnmower? A lawnmower belches fumes and splits the peace with its roars and pollutes the air and endangers toes and sucks up fossil fuel and dispenses migraines . . . and you have to do it all over again later in the week!

How come homeowners don't have to apply to Stratford City Council for permission to inflict a *lawnmower* on their neighbours?

Hard to figure, but then as I said, people and lawns are a bad combination for rationality.

As the mayor of Stratford, Dave Hunt, said, following the decision: "I hope we won't get flooded with people who are going to want chicken coops and things in their yards."

Well, exactly. 'Cause you know what chicken coops lead to, don't you?

Eggs.

Certs Is a Dog Mint

I want to write a word or two about . . . dog breath.

Yes, Dog Breath. Oh, like you, I never thought of dog breath as a major concern of anybody this side of another dog caught downwind . . . but I've been educated. I've had my eyes opened. I can thank my faithful four-footed semi-Australian shepherd Rufus for the enlightenment. He did it in that typical, no-frills, straight-ahead style he has.

He breathed on me.

Whuff! That's bad. I've been in waste-disposal facilities. I've been in chicken coops. I've been in a Munich beer tent following Oktoberfest and I've been in a high-density public restroom on the outskirts of Cuernavaca . . . and I'd put Rufus's breath up against any or all of the above. He's got breath that could kill plants. Blister paint. Weld base metals. Rufus has baaaaaad breath.

I know why it's so bad, of course. It's because Rufus eats anything that moves and several things that don't. I won't elaborate because you may be eating, but trust me. Rufus is a fur-bearing garburator. He gobbles stuff you wouldn't handle without a radiation suit and a pair of tongs.

My vet says I'm all wet about this. He says dog breath — sorry, canine halitosis — like human halitosis, is caused by tartar buildup, or "people food" getting caught between the dog's teeth. Her solution? She says a good cleaning and scraping usually gives a pooch back his inoffensive puppy breath.

Couple of problems, though . . . number one, it's a little difficult to visualize Rufus sitting in a dentist chair wearing a bib and opening wide while the vet picks and probes around. So that means a general anaesthetic would be required. Overall cost: anywhere from $100 to $200.

And it's not likely that a post-operative Rufus is suddenly going to start practising good dental hygiene, right? He's unlikely to avoid suspect food groups or take up flossing. So this is an expense that would be incurred on a fairly regular basis.

That's another thing my vet tells me — it's my responsibility to look after Rufus's teeth. She says Rufus should have his teeth brushed after every meal.

To which I could only respond, Yeah, right! For one thing, I couldn't cover the cost of the toothpaste. Rufus eats about 279 meals a day. For another thing, Rufus weighs eighty-five pounds and he's got jaws like a Louisiana bull alligator. Sure, he's easygoing most of the time, but those are sharp teeth we're talking about brushing vigorously. I'm not going in there armed with nothing more lethal than a Pic O Pay.

Instead I've hit on a dietary additive. I've sneaked it into Rufus's daily menu. Costs me a fortune but I've probably got the only dog in the world addicted to Certs.

Now if I could just teach him to suck, not gobble. . . .

"Meow" Is Catspeak for "Waiter!"

I ever tell you about my cat? I've got one. A fourteen-year-old motley-pelted furbag with battle-scarred ears and a don't-tread-on-me stare. Name's Lassie. Yeah, well, that's what you get when you turn to your five-year-old son and say, "What do you think we should call our brand new little kitty cat, Dan?"

Lassie. A fourteen-year-old error in judgement. In that fourteen years, Dan's turned into an adult and moved out to go to college. Lassie's turned into a housebound wolverine that a Swat Team of bailiffs couldn't budge.

Did I say we HAVE a cat named Lassie? How silly. We don't HAVE a cat named Lassie. A cat named Lassie shares our house. We get to open cans of Meow Chow and wash the cat dish and perform latrine duty on the litter box and replace shredded armchairs and chesterfields from time to time. And in return Lassie does . . . absolutely nothing. That's what cats do best. Garrison Keillor wrote that cats are intended to teach us that not everything in nature has a function.

Well, I think cats are intended to teach us a lot of things, humility being at the forefront. Somebody else once observed that bullies can never abide cats. I think that's probably true, too, because cats can't be bullied. Cats won't cower like a dog or flutter like a budgie or squeal like a pig or whinny like a horse. You can yell at them, kick at them, throw the kitchen microwave at them, and all you'll get for your troubles is that haughty "up yours" feline glare.

I hate to admit it — and I never would in front of Lassie — but you have to respect cats in the end. They aren't robust or rambunctious like dogs but they're a helluva lot smarter. A dog will chase and fetch a stick all day long. Try throwing one for a cat sometime. The cat will watch the stick arc through the air, then lazily turn its eyes on you as if to say, "Let me get this straight: you've thrown this stick and now you're waiting for me to run after it and bring it back to you? Nooooo, I think not."

Sometimes . . . often it's in the middle of the night when I'm shuffling off barefoot to the bathroom and feel my foot slither across a cold, wet Lassie-generated hairball . . . sometimes I reflect on the irony that the last fourteen years needn't have been this way. Way back when he was a kitten, a neighbour (not a well woman) actually fell in love with Lassie. Offered to buy him from me. No, no, I said. Couldn't do that. Family pet, you know. Imagine that . . . someone willing to pay money for Lassie. And I turned her down.

Reminds me of my favourite cat story. An antiques expert is strolling through Yorkville in Toronto when he sees a scruffy old cat in a store window lapping milk out of what he recognizes is a crusty but priceless Ming dynasty saucer. This saucer he knows is worth thousands of dollars. The guy looks around, straightens his tie, slicks back his hair, and goes into the shop. "Say," he says to the shopkeeper, "I kind of took a shine to that old cat in the window. I'll give ya five bucks for him."

"No, sorry," says the shopkeeper. "The cat's not for sale." The antiques buyer panics, says, "Look, uhh . . . I really need that cat. I've, ahhh, got a lot of mice in my apartment. I'll give you fifty bucks for him."

Shopkeeper rolls his eyes and says, "Fifty bucks — sold!" And the antiques buyer says, "Listen, I was wondering, you know, for that fifty bucks could you throw in that crummy old saucer? That way I won't have to buy another dish."

Shopkeeper shakes his head. "Sorry, man, that's my lucky saucer. So far this week it's sold thirty-seven cats."

See? You're laughing. But I told that joke to Lassie and he didn't crack a smile.

The Natives
Are Restless

Ever wonder what we humans did to deserve first place? To be in the catbird seat, I mean? On the planet, species-wise.

Think about it. You and I can't soar like eagles or swim like porpoises or run like cheetahs or climb like lowland gorillas. Hand for paw and tooth for claw, we're no match for grizzlies, elephants, water buffalo, pit vipers, tigers, or tiger sharks. Our muscles are dinky, our talons and incisors laughable. We're not cunning enough to chase down a meal barehanded or hardy enough to spend a night in the bush bare naked without developing pleurisy or worse.

Let's face it — as far as innate abilities go, we humans should be in the zoo, and zebras, giraffes, and moray eels should be paying admission to look at *us*.

Could happen, too. Don't like to wax apocalyptic on you, but a careful perusal of the media and the threading together of two or three seemingly unconnected news stories make me wonder if the animals aren't getting restless and Homo sapiens' days aren't numbered.

Consider the case of Mark and Cathy Peterson, of Olathe, Kansas. Happily married until . . . they began to notice odd and inexplicable happenings in their apartment. Such as finding, each morning when they rose, strange marks . . . almost like treadmarks crisscrossing on the kitchen floor. Then there were those eerie crashes in the night.

One night Mark was sitting quietly reading at the kitchen table late at night when he heard a furtive rustling down by the bottom of the refrigerator. As he watched in horror, Mark could make out a head coming around the corner of the kitchen cupboard along the floor. First the head . . . then the neck . . . then . . . more neck . . . and then — well, an *awful* lot of neck, really. Turned out upon investigation that

Mark and Cathy Peterson had been sharing their apartment with a three-foot python, left behind by a previous tenant.

Hey. They're a little spooky, I grant you, but they don't claw the furniture and they don't bark. Betcha the folks who live on Chestnut Avenue in Halifax would have traded their problem for one slightly used three-foot python. Their problem was crows. Eight of them. They took over Chestnut Street as sure as Marlon Brando and his boys invaded Wrightsville in the movie *The Wild One*. The feathered octet patrolled the street for several days, dive-bombing hapless pedestrians and terrorizing cats and dogs. Kids going out to play wore safety hats and bicycle helmets. One woman was buzzed while hanging out her wash — buzzed close enough to knock her glasses off. Aerial crow attacks in Halifax and phantom pythons in Kansas in the same week — mere coincidence? I think not.

And neither would Steve Yellich. Steve lives in a log cabin on the outskirts of Smithers, British Columbia. He was sitting peaceably on the tailgate of his pickup watching the sun go down one night recently. But when he stood up to go inside, something had a hold of his leg. Steve looked down and saw . . . a savage furry beast with its huge teeth clamped on his ankle. Steve is seventy-one and has had a stroke; consequently, he carries a sawed-off hockey stick to get around. And he still has a pretty good slap shot. Steve whomped his assailant on the head, whereupon the creature transferred its crazed attentions to the hockey stick. "I was swinging him around," recalls Steve, "he plopped on his back and started to come at me and I slugged him again. If I didn't have a stick, he could have bit both my legs off like nothing. You should have seen his teeth."

And what was the creature that nearly turned our two-legged hero into a one-legged one? It was . . . a *beaver*.

Yes. The cuddly, placid, docile mascot of our cuddly, placid, docile nation. "Never heard of such an attack before," mused a B.C. wildlife officer.

Well, get used to it I say. The animals are fed up with our planetary mismanagement and they're not going to take it anymore. Yesterday the Soviet Union, the Tories, and the NDP — tomorrow?

Who knows. But remember to walk softly. Especially when the cat's in the room. And carry a big stick.

A goalie stick if you can get one.